Vinegar, Oil, and Alcohol

PICKLED

Delicacies

Schiffer Publishing Ltd®

4880 Lower Valley Road • Atglen, PA 19310

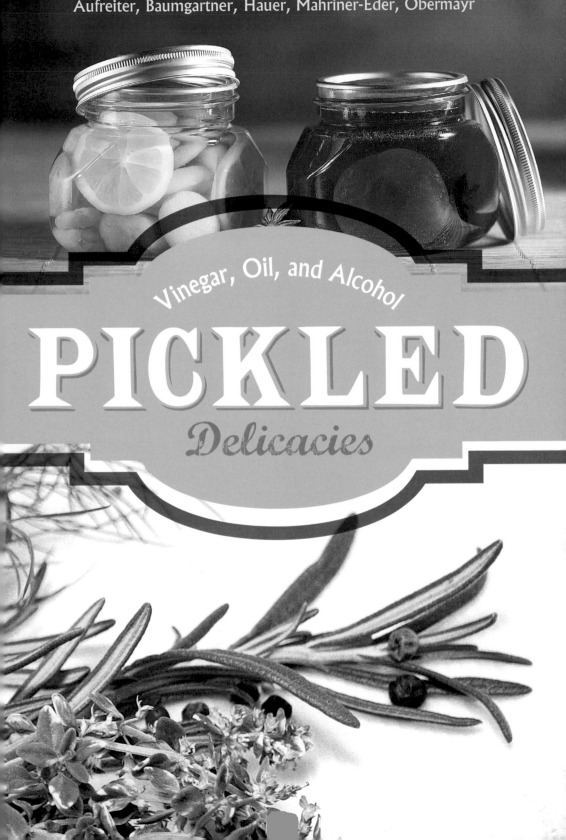

Aufreiter, Baumgartner, Hauer, Mahriner-Eder, Obermayr

Vinegar, Oil, and Alcohol

PICKLED

Delicacies

Other Schiffer Books on Related Subjects:
Aroma Kitchen: Cooking with Essential Oils, Sabine Hönig and Ursula Kutschera, 978-0-7643-4793-1

Cooking with Mustard: Empowering Your Palate, G. Poggenpohl, 978-0-7643-3643-0

Garnishing & Decorating: Ideas for all Seasons, Georg Hartung and Thomas Schultze, 978-0-7643-4627-9

Originally published as Eingelegte Köstlichkeiten
by Leopold Stocker Verlag, Graz, Austria & Stuttgart, Germany
© 2008 by Leopold Stocker Verlag, Graz
Translated from the German by Jonee Tiedemann

Cover design by Brenda McCallum
Type set in Albertus Medium/Helvetica Narrow

ISBN: 978-0-7643-4872-3
Printed in China

Published by Schiffer Publishing, Ltd.
4880 Lower Valley Road
Atglen, PA 19310
Phone: (610) 593-1777; Fax: (610) 593-2002
E-mail: Info@schifferbooks.com

For our complete selection of fine books on this and related subjects,
please visit our website at www.schifferbooks.com. You may also write for a free catalog.

This book may be purchased from the publisher. Please try your bookstore first.

We are always looking for people to write books on new and related subjects.
If you have an idea for a book, please contact us at proposals@schifferbooks.com.

Schiffer Publishing's titles are available at special discounts for bulk purchases for sales promotions or premiums. Special editions, including personalized covers, corporate imprints, and excerpts can be created in large quantities for special needs. For more information, contact the publisher.

Contents

Contents

Preface

With our book *Pickled Delicacies*, we invite you to discover pickled foods in all of their variety (again). This book should entice you to have fun preparing pickled delicacies for yourself and others.

We have packaged local fruits and vegetables, fish, eggs, and a few tasty and vitamin-rich delicacies in vinegar, oil, alcohol, or salt. Many of our products have become popular gifts among our friends and family—perhaps because we are also giving away something valuable, which is time and effort.

We have spent many enjoyable hours creating and tasting the recipes, some of which have unusual ingredients.

We hope you have as much fun as we did as you try out our recipes. We encourage you to let your fantasy run freely and not merely follow the recipes. You will be surprised at the original results. If you are not yet a professional pickler, our book is a good introduction. We have compiled a detailed list of ingredients and preparation tips while you take your first steps.

The authors wish you all the best as you try out these recipes.

Good to know ...

It used to be necessary to lay in a supply of non-perishable food for the winter months. Our recipes have not necessarily been selected based on the supplies you might have in your pantry; rather, culinary experimentation is the main goal here. We know from experience that a small but select stash of original delicacies goes a long way toward providing that special something for both planned and improvised lunches and dinners. This book should become your trusted partner in all things related to pickled delicacies. Select delicacies from our book can make a special buffet. Just add a loaf of fresh bread or baguettes and make sure you have a good selection of beverages on hand.

The book is divided into five chapters based on type of pickling:

- Pickling in alcohol
- Pickling in vinegar
- Pickling in oil
- Pickling in salt
- Pickling in sugar

As you may guess, the emphasis is on pickling in alcohol, pickling in vinegar, and pickling in oil. The final two chapters on pickling in salt and sugar include a small but select recipe collection.

Recipes in each chapter are divided into fruits, vegetables, fish, and eggs. Included are tips on how to modify the ingredients for specific delicacies, since individual tastes differ. You can vary both the amounts and the ingredients.

Depending on the size of your jars and bottles, the required amount of fluid may vary from recipe to recipe. You can use leftover pickling juice for salads, preserves, and other foods.

Keep in mind that tablespoons and teaspoons indicate level tablespoons and teaspoons. Sugar refers to granulated sugar unless otherwise specified. The amounts for herbs always refer to fresh herbs unless otherwise indicated.

And now, let's get started ...

The first step to achieving the desired result is to select and prepare the containers. It is important to choose containers that meet the following requirements:

1. convenient
2. appealing appearance
3. heat resistant
4. acid resistant
5. undamaged
6. can be closed firmly
7. easy to clean

We suggest that you only use jars with a twisting lid or snap lid. Bottles are best closed with a matching cork. Make sure you fill the bottle to about an inch below the rim. Press the cork into the neck of the bottle so that only about a quarter-inch sticks out.

Appealing jars, glasses, and bottles can be found in specialty retail shops and warehouses. Take every opportunity to acquire jars and bottles. This way you always have one handy if you want to make a nice present, or a special deal might entice you to purchase a larger number of them.

The jars and bottles must be thoroughly washed with hot water and detergent before they are used. It is best to use a round brush for this. Don't forget to rinse the containers with plenty of hot water. Of course you can clean the jars in the dishwasher, too.

Then sterilize the jars and bottles. Place the containers into a deep, wide pot (perhaps onto a removable grid). Fill the pot with water and make sure the jars and bottles are completely covered and don't touch each other. Bring the water to a boil and let the jars boil for 10 minutes. Carefully remove the containers and let them dry face down on a clean kitchen cloth. The lids, rubber seals, and corks also need to be boiled for a few minutes. Cover the containers with a clean cloth until they are used.

Sterilize the jars and let them drain.

Choose the ingredients carefully. Only impeccable fruits, vegetables, fish, and eggs should be made into pickled delicacies. Check the appearance, freshness, smell, and taste. Fruits and vegetables should be neither underripe nor overripe. Even if you cut away these sections, it will compromise the result. It would be a pity to put so much time and effort into something that did not turn out well. Use only the freshest fish and eggs. Fresh fish has clear and bulging eyes, intensely red gills, a clean smell, tight skin, and no pressure marks. If the fish has been cleaned already, the cut surfaces must be white, juicy, and firm.

Check the markets for appealing possibilities.

As to eggs, perform the swimming test to determine if they are suitable: Fill a large glass bowl with plenty of cold water and put the eggs into it. A fresh egg remains on the bottom in a horizontal position. An egg that is two to three weeks old rises up, with the thick end up. Older eggs float on the surface.

To enjoy your homemade delicacies for a long time, be careful how you store them. Cleanliness while preparing and storing, the right storage conditions, and continuous control of the items are the most important factors.

The following tips will help you to keep the food fresh:

1. Follow the storage directions.
2. If you are making large amounts or many different delicacies, label them with the name and date.
3. Check regularly to make sure the containers are tightly sealed.
4. Once you open a jar, keep it in the refrigerator and consume the content soon. Make only as much as you will eat in the near future. Vinegars and oils are an exception.
5. If you discover mold or rot, discard the products.

Tips and techniques

Blanching

Blanching is important in conserving vegetables and fruits. This step eliminates many of the enzymes that cause rot and discoloration, thereby prolonging their shelf life. Place the vegetables or fruits into a wire basket and dip them into a large pot with boiling water. Make sure that the water continues to boil as quickly as possible after immersion. Boil the fruits or vegetables for three minutes. Remove the basket and empty the contents into a bowl of ice water, or rinse the blanched items under running cold water. Drain well. If you do not have a wire basket handy, place the vegetables directly into the boiling water and remove them with a sieve after blanching.

Filtering

When preparing vinegars and oils it may be necessary to strain out spices and other residue. This is best done with a cheesecloth or coffee filter. Place the cheesecloth inside a sieve, or the coffee filter into a funnel. Pour in the liquid slowly. For some recipes, you will have to replace the filter or cheesecloth several times.

Blanching with a wire basket (left)
Cooling in ice water (right)

Glazing

Glaze the items until they become translucent but not too soft.

Holding pickled items under liquid

When pickling, it is important that the food items remain submerged under the liquid. To hold down foods that tend to float, purchase some wooden craft sticks. Cut them to fit inside the jar and cross two pieces over each other above the items. If you place the sticks briefly into boiling water, they are more flexible.

Keep food submerged
with wooden craft sticks

Julienne

Cut vegetables into ¼-inch-thick and 1½-inch-long slices.

Reducing

Liquid is boiled over a long period of time to reduce it and intensify the flavors.

Saltwater

Prepare saltwater by adding 1 tablespoon salt to 4 cups of water and bringing it to a boil. The water should have a slightly salty taste.

Simmering

Cook the food items in gently boiling liquid.

Spice bags, or spices in a tea ball, make it easy to remove spices after they've done their job of flavoring the liquid.

Spice bags

Spices and herbs are easily removed from boiling liquid if they are placed inside a small bag or tea ball. You can use a ready-made tea ball or make a gauze bag. Place the recommended spices and/or herbs into the center of a 6×6-inch gauze cloth, pull the corners together, and tie with a piece of yarn.

Steaming

Cooking food with steam. You'll need a pot with a sieve insert; water should just reach the sieve.

Syrup

Syrup is a concentrated, thick solution of sugar and water, fruit juices, or plant extracts. It is prepared by boiling sugar solutions over a long period on low heat.

Zests

Zests are thin slices from the peels of oranges, lemons, and limes. They are made with a zest peeler or a small, pointed knife.

Zests are best cut using a
zest peeler

Pickling A-Z

Allspice
Tastes like a mix of cinnamon, cloves, nutmeg, and pepper.

Armagnac
A high-quality French brandy produced from wine spirits of the Armagnac region.

Bourbon
An American whiskey.

Calvados
A French apple brandy produced mostly in the Normandy reglon.

Cardamom
Has a nice, spicy taste and harmonizes well with exotic spices such as cinnamon, cloves, or nutmeg.

Cider
Fermented apple or pear juice.

Clementines
Mandarins without seeds. They are cultivated mainly in Egypt, Algeria, Morocco, Spain, and Italy.

Cloves
Harmonize well with cinnamon and cardamom. For salty dishes you should also add pepper, bay leaf, or onions.

Cumin
Has a slightly smokey, appealing taste.

Dill umbel
The umbrella-shaped flower of the dill herb.

Eggplant
These pumpkin-shaped vegetables are either violet or green. They contain a natural poison that is destroyed when they are heated.

Gin
A distillate from barley and rye combined with juniper berries and spices.

Ginger
Its taste is quite intense and highly aromatic.

Grappa
An Italian term for a pomace brandy.

Herring, green
Fresh, untreated herring.

Hyssop
Has a slightly bitter taste and must be used with care. It is used for salads, soups, and sauces.

Kirsch (cherry brandy)
A distillate made from cherry mash.

Lemon balm
Has a lemon-like smell and a nice spicy taste.

Lime
Has a thin, yellow-green or yellow skin that tears easily. The round or oval fruits have a sour, juicy, yellow to yellow-greenish pulp.

Mace (nutmeg flower)
The dried seed husk of nutmeg. Mace flowers have a finer taste than the sweet, aromatic nutmeg.

Madeira
A dessert wine from the Portuguese island of Madeira. It is produced with white wine, which is spirited with grape distillates. Wines are spirited to increase their alcohol content and to keep the wine sweet by suppressing the fermentation.

Oregano
Also called wild marjoram, has a delicate aroma similar to marjoram.

Papayas
Shaped like longish melons. The orange pulp tastes like melon.

Pecans
Sweeter, contain more oil, and are more aromatic than walnuts.

Piri piri
Small, hot, bright-red Capsicum peppers. You can use piri piri fresh or dried, cut into small pieces, or ground.

Quinces
Fruits from the quince tree, shaped between an apple and a pear. The taste is sour, sometimes bitter. The pulp is hard and cannot be consumed raw.

Sour cherries
A type of cherry with a sour taste

Star anise
Smells like aniseed, however its taste is fuller and fierier.

Scallops
The firm meat is delicious, nut-like, and slightly sweet, with a round taste.

Tarragon

Its longish leaves taste slightly spicy and aromatic, with a hint of pepper and slightly bitter.

Thyme

Smells spicy and goes well with bay leaves, nutmeg, rosemary, and sage. It contains antibacterial components.

Turmeric

Belongs to the ginger plant group.

Veltliner

An Austrian grape variety from the wine regions of Kamptal, Kremstal, Donauland, and the Wachau.

Xeres wine

A Spanish dessert wine in the sherry family.

Vinegar, Oil, and Alcohol

PICKLED

Delicacies

Pickling in Alcohol

Fruits in alcohol

Pineapple in white rum

3 cups white rum
2 large, ripe pineapples
1–2 cinnamon sticks
2–3 tablespoons honey

Peel the pineapple and remove the tough sections, then cut into four or eight pieces. Make sure you cut out the hard center generously. Then cut the four or eight pieces into chunks, mix with the honey, and put into the jars. Place the cinnamon sticks between the pineapple chunks and add the rum. The rum must be about a finger's width above the pineapple at the top. Close tightly and leave in a cold place to soak for about four weeks.

Apple-grape secret

1 ½ cups apple brandy
1 cup apple juice
½ cup apple cider vinegar
4 cups sour apples
2 cups blue grapes
¾ cup sugar
juice of 1 lemon
1 vanilla bean
¾-inch fresh ginger root

Peel the apples, cut into quarters, and remove the center. Then cut the quarters in half in both directions and immediately place into a bowl with lemon water so they don't turn brown. Wash and drain the grapes, and pluck them from the stems. Cut the vanilla bean into several pieces. Peel the ginger root and grate coarsely.

Stack the fruit in the jars, alternating with the ginger and the vanilla pieces. Heat the apple juice with the apple cider vinegar, apple brandy, and sugar until the sugar has dissolved. Fill the jars with the hot mix, close tightly, and store in a cool place.

Pineapple in white rum (left)
Apple-grape secret (right)

Pineapple in kirsch

Peel the pineapple and remove the tough sections and core. Cut into slices and put into
the jar with the cinnamon, orange peel, sugar, and almonds. Fill the jar with kirsch and
close tightly. Store in a cool, dark place for two to three months. Shake during the first
couple of weeks so the sugar dissolves.

2 cups kirsch
1 ripe pineapple
½ to ¾ cup coarse sugar
2 cinnamon sticks
2 strips of orange peel
3 almonds

〉 Tip

The jar looks especially attractive when you position the pineapple slices so that the
center hole is visible.

Apples in wine

Boil water and sugar vigorously in a large, wide pot for about 10 minutes, uncovered.
Peel the apples, cut out the core, and add to the sugar syrup, boiling gently for 5 minutes.
Do not overfill the pot with apples. Remove the apples with a skimmer and drain. Stack
the apples in a jar and add the cloves and cinnamon stick. Mix ¼ cup of the sugar syrup
with the wine, schnapps, and lemon juice and pour over the apples to cover. Close tightly
and store in a cool place. We recommend that you eat them soon.

3 cups white wine
1 cup water
½ cup apple schnaps
5 cups small apples, or
 about 8 apples
2 cups sugar
5 cloves
1 cinnamon stick
2 tablespoons lemon
 juice

Pears in vodka

Wash and dry the pears, and pierce in several places. Place the fruit into the jar and
add the sugar and spliced vanilla bean. Cover with the vodka. Close tightly and store
in a cool, dark place for three to four months. Shake during the first few weeks so the
sugar dissolves.

4¼ cups vodka
3–4 ripe pears
1¼ –1¾ cups coarse sugar
1 vanilla bean

〉 Tip

If you like it sweet, increase the amount of sugar to 2 cups.

Pears in saffron syrup

1 cup white wine
¾ cup water
4 firm pears
½ cup sugar
1 vanilla bean
1 bag of saffron
1 tablespoon orange
   water (boil an orange
   peel in sugar water)

Wash the pears, peel, quarter, and remove pits and core. Slice the vanilla bean lengthwise, scrape out the pulp, and set aside the pulp for later. Boil the wine, water, and sugar until the sugar has dissolved. Then add the vanilla pulp and saffron and boil gently for 15 minutes. Now add the orange water and pear quarters and boil until they are semi-soft. Remove the fruit with the skimmer and place into jars. Pour the hot syrup over it and add the vanilla bean. Close tightly and store in a cool place.

> ❱ Tip

Because of their beautiful color, pears in saffron syrup make a great decorative dessert. Serve this delicacy with ice cream or pudding, or use it as an original cake topping. Put a thin layer of jam on a cake base and decorate with thinly sliced, well-drained pears. If you don't plan to serve the cake right away, cover the pears with jelly.

Pears in red wine

1½ cups red wine
½ cup water
2½ pounds small pears
1 cup sugar
1 tablespoon juniper
   berries
4 allspice berries
1 piece of orange peel
1 cinnamon stick

Wash the pears, peel, cut out the core, and slice. Boil the juniper berries, allspice berries, orange peel, and cinnamon stick with the sugar and water. Steam the pears in this liquid until tender, but not mushy. Drain well and place in previously prepared jars. Let the liquid boil for another 5 minutes and pour over the fruit. Close the jars tightly. We recommend consuming the pears soon.

Pears in saffron syrup (left)
Pears in red wine (right)

Strawberries in Madeira

Wash, drain, and stem the strawberries and place in a jar. Boil the sugar and water until the sugar has dissoved. Cool, mix with Madeira, and pour over the strawberries to cover. Close tightly and allow to rest for several days.

2 cups Madeira
½ cup water
2 cups strawberries
1¼ cups sugar

> ❱ Tip

Strawberries in madeira are great with ice cream, pudding, and other sweet dishes.

Strawberries in Madeira (left), and with ice cream, a special treat (right)

Figs in bourbon

Cut the figs in half and place in jars with the rock sugar. Add the sliced vanilla bean and fill with bourbon. Close tightly and leave in a sunny place for about three months before serving. Shake occasionally.

½ cup bourbon
1 cup dried figs
4 teaspoons brown rock sugar
1 vanilla bean

Figs in bourbon

Clementines in whiskey

3 cups whiskey

4 tablespoons water

1 pound clementines
(weigh without
the peel

1 cup sugar

Peel the clementines and carefully remove the white skin. Cut into slices. Heat the water and sugar until it has dissolved. Briefly place the clementines into the sugar solution, turn carefully, and let cool. Fill the jar, add the whiskey, close tightly and let sit for at least for 4 weeks before consuming them.

Kumquats in brandy

3 cups brandy

½ cup water

2 pounds kumquats

4 oranges with high juice
content

1½ cups sugar

pulp of one vanilla bean

½ cinnamon stick

Wash the kumquats thoroughly under running water, dry, and prick each one several times with a toothpick. Press out the oranges and strain the juice. Cut the vanilla bean lengthwise and scrape out the pulp.

Boil the orange juice, vanilla pulp, cinnamon stick, sugar, and water over medium heat for about 5 minutes. Place the kumquats one-by-one into the boiling liquid and boil for about 5 minutes. Remove and stack into jars. Strain the liquid and reduce to about half on high heat. Let cool and pour into the glasses. Fill the glasses with brandy, close tightly, and store in a cool, dark place. Let sit at least 1 month before serving.

> ❯ Tip

Until a few years ago, the evergreen kumquat shrubs were mostly known as decorative plants. Recently, people have started to appreciate the fruit's tart taste. Kumquats are usually available during the winter months and are grown in Israel, Morocco, Spain, South Africa, and South America. They can be consumed with their skin. Our recipe uses them for sweet desserts and as a side dish for roasts and ragouts. You can use kumquats to pep up your Christmas fruit cake. Kumquats are also used in leafy salads, jams, chutney, and liqueur. They can also be candied. Top your pancakes with kumquats in brandy.

Kumquats in brandy (left)
Clementines in whiskey (right)

Grappa grapes

Wash the grapes thoroughly and drain on paper towels.

Carefully mix the cleaned grapes with the sugar, cover, and let sit overnight in a cool place.

Wash and dry the raisins, and mix with the grape and sugar mix. Divide into jars and fill with grappa. Close the jars tightly and store in a cool, dry place for 2–4 months.

3 cups grappa
1⅓ pounds blue grapes
1⅓ pounds green grapes
5 cups sugar
4 teaspoons raisins

❱ Tip

Grappa grapes add a special touch to many sweet dishes.

Cranberries in red wine

Boil the cranberries with the red wine, sugar, and orange zest for about 10 minutes, then pour into twist-cap jars.

¾ cup red wine
4 cups cranberries
¾ cup sugar
a few strips of orange zest

Grappa grapes: grape variation: grapes, raisins, grappa

Cranberries in red wine: a great side dish for venison

Apricots in white rum

1–2 cups white rum
2 cups dried apricots
¼ lemon
½ cup white rock sugar

Pour boiling water over the apricots until they are completely covered. Let soak about 1 hour. Remove the fruit and dry well. Wash the lemon thoroughly and cut into thin slices. Place the apricots, lemon slices, and rock sugar in the jar in alternating layers. Fill with white rum to about 2 inches over the fruit, then close the jar tightly. Store in a sunny place until the rock sugar has dissolved, and shake occasionally.

Honey plums

2¼ pounds plums
3 cups dry white wine
1 cinnamon stick
2 cloves
2 pieces star anise
¾ cup honey, divided

Wash the plums and prick them a few times with a toothpick so they won't crack. Boil the white wine, spices, and 3 tablespoons of honey. Add the plums and soak for 2–3 minutes. Remove the fruit and place into a prepared jar. Reduce the remaining fluid by almost half and remove from the stove. Add the remaining honey, mix, and pour while warm over the plums. Allow it to soak in the refrigerator for at least 1 day and serve within 1 week.

> ❯ Tip

Serve the honey plums with sweet souffles. If the fruits are large, cut them in half and remove the pit after heating them.

Apricots in white rum (left)
Honey plums (right)

Quinces with cinnamon

Use a cloth to rub off the quinces' white coating, then wash them thorougly. Peel, cut in half, and remove the core. Put half a quince, the peels, and the core into boiling water. Boil for about 45 minutes, remove, strain, and add to the water again. Mix the wine with sugar, cinnamon stick, and the quince brew. Add the quince halves and boil until they are soft. Use a skimmer to remove the fruit, pile into jars, and cover with the brew. Best to consume soon.

1¼ cups white wine
1¼ cups water
3⅓ pounds quinces
1–1¼ cups sugar
1 cinnamon stick

Pears in ginger gin

Douse the pears with boiling water and let sit for a moment. Shock with cold water, peel, cut in half, and remove pits. Place the pears into a bowl and spread sugar-ginger mix over it. Cover and leave for 24 hours in a cool place. Then pile the fruit into jars and fill with gin. Close the jars tightly.

3¼ cups gin
2¼ pounds peaches
1½ to 1¾ cups sugar
1½ teaspoons ground ginger

Peaches in brandy

Blanch, peel, and remove the pits from the peaches. Boil water with 2 cups of sugar; remove foam if necessary and boil for 5 minutes at low heat. Place the peaches carefully into the sugar solution, bring to a boil, and simmer for 5 minutes. Remove the fruit with a skimmer and cool. Boil the remaining sugar with 2½ cups of the brew and a spice bag consisting of the vanilla bean, cinnamon stick, and the cardomom seeds, 10 minutes. Let cool a bit and add the brandy.

Use tootpicks to stick half a candy cherry into each peach half, and place them into a glass jar. Remove the spice bag and pour the syrup over the peaches until they are covered. Shake the glass carefully so air bubbles can escape. Close tightly and let rest for at least two weeks before serving.

1¼ cups brandy
4¼ cups water
3⅓ pounds firm peaches
5 cups sugar, divided
½ cup candied cherries, cut in half
1 vanilla bean
1 cinnamon stick
6 cloves
optional: 3 cardamom pods

❯ Tip

Peaches in brandy are delicious even without the candy cherries and cardamom.

Quinces in calvados

1½ cups calvados
1 cup white wine
½ cup lemon juice
2¼ pounds quinces
2 cups coarse sugar
1 cinnamon stick
⅓-inch fresh ginger root
3 cloves
1 piece star anise

Rub off the fruit's white coating with a cloth, wash thoroughly, and drain. Peel the quinces thinly and cut into thin slices; remove large pits. Rinse the sliced fruits with lemon juice and let soak for about 30 minutes.

Boil the white wine and sugar, stirring, over medium heat. Make a spice bag from the cinnamon stick pieces, chopped ginger root, star anise, and cloves, and add to the pot. Let the quinces soak in the gently boiling wine brew, stirring occasionally. Remove the quinces with a skimmer and carefully put them into jars. Remove the spice bag, reduce the brew to a thick syrup, and pour over the fruit. Fill the jars with calvados and close tightly.

Sour cherries in cherry spirit

4¼ cups cherry brandy
3¼ cups water
4⅓ pounds sour cherries
3 cups sugar
pulp of 1 vanilla bean
1 cinnamon stick

Wash and dry the sour cherries and put into a prepared jar with the spices. Boil the water with the sugar and allow to cool. Then pour the sugar syrup and the cherry spirit over the sour cherries and close the jar. Store in a sunny place for about 1 week, and then store in a cool and dark place.

Quinces in calvados (left)
Peaches in brandy (right)

Sour cherries in vodka

Wash and dry the sour cherries and remove the stems. Fill the glasses, alternating with crushed rock sugar and the sour cherries. Cut a thin slice of lemon peel into small pieces and mix with the crushed cinnamon stick. Fill with the vodka, close tightly, and leave to soak for at least 8 weeks.

4¼ cups vodka
2¼ pounds sour cherries
1 cup rock sugar (white is best)
1 cinnamon stick
1 slice of lemon peel

Sherry cherries

Remove the stems from the cherries, wash, and remove pits. The fruits should remain fairly intact. Bring to a boil the sherry, water, sugar, vanilla sugar, cloves, allspice berries, and orange peel, and simmer for about 5 minutes, stirring occasionally. Strain the brew and add the cherry brandy. You might want to add more sugar. Put the cherries into the jars and fill with the hot brew. Cool, close the jars, and keep refrigerated. Best if consumed soon.

¾ cup sherry
2–3 tablespoons cherry brandy
¼ cup water
1 pound cherries, weigh without pits
½ cup sugar
2 packs of vanilla sugar
2 cloves
2 allspice berries
1 piece of orange peel

Sour cherries in vodka (left) and sherry cherries (right)

Rum plums

rum (38% ABV),
    as needed
1 lemon
2 tablespoons ground
    cloves
1 cinnamon stick
1 vanilla bean
2 cups water
2 cups sugar
2 cups pitted dried plums
½ cup raisins

Thinly slice the lemon. Put the ground cloves, cinnamon stick, sliced vanilla bean, lemon slices, and sugar in the water. Bring to a boil and reduce it to a syrup, while stirring. Add the dried plums and raisins and let cool overnight. Put the mix into jars and fill with enough rum so that the fruit is covered. Close tightly. Let soak about 2 weeks before serving.

❱ Tip

Not only are these rum plums a delicacy during the Christmas season, they are a fantastic treat during the entire year. Cover the rum plums with chocolate and treat your loved ones to something truly delicious.

Rum prunes

1 cup rum (80% ABV)
1 pound plums
1¼ cup sugar

Wash the prunes under cold water and carefully dry with a cloth. Pile the fruit and sugar into a large jar and fill with rum. Close tightly and store in a cool place. Allow it to sit at least 2 months before consuming.

❱ Tip

Use only top-quality prunes, and do not remove the pits. Use enough rum so that the prunes are covered completely. If they float to the top, hold them in place with wooden spatula handles (page 16).

Plums in red wine

1 cup red wine
2¼ pounds plums
1 cup red wine vinegar
4 cups sugar
½ cinnamon stick
2 cloves
bay leaf
1 pinch ground nutmeg

Wash and dry the plums and prick them with a needle. Boil them with the remaining ingredients for about 10 minutes, then place the plums in a jar. Continue to simmer the brew for about 20 minutes. Pour the brew over the plums while still hot, allow to cool down, and close the jar tightly. Let sit at least 4 months before serving.

Prunes in red wine

Heat the red wine with the cinnamon stick and sugar. Turn off the heat and add the prepared prunes, allowing them to soak for about an hour. Remove the cinnamon bark, heat again (without boiling), and put the hot mixture into the jars.

3¼ cups red wine
1 cinnamon stick
1½ cup sugar
1¼ pound plums without pits

❯ Tip

Serve the prunes in red wine with sweet dishes such as souffles.

Lemons in vodka

Wash the lemons, cut into thin slices, and pile into jars, alternating with the washed mint leaves. Boil the sugar and water to make a syrup, allow to cool, and mix with the vodka. Pour the brew over the lemon slices and close the jars. The lemons are ready to eat after 2 weeks.

1¾ cup vodka
2 pounds lemons
25 peppermint leaves
1¼ cup sugar
1¼ cup water

❯ Tip

Serve this compote with smoked or fried fish.

Plums in red wine (left)
Lemons in vodka (right)

Plums with candied ginger

¾ cup red wine
2¼ pounds plums
1 tablespoon candied
   ginger, finely chopped
¾ cup water
1 cup brown rock sugar
½ vanilla bean

Wash and dry the plums, remove the stems, and place into jars with the candied ginger. Boil the red wine with the water, rock sugar, and sliced vanilla bean, stirring until the sugar has dissolved. Allow the mixture to cool and remove the vanilla bean. Pour the brew over the plums, close the jars, and store in a cool place. Best if served soon.

Sour cherries in wine

4¼ cups red wine
½ cup rum
3⅓ pounds sour cherries
3¼ cups sugar
1 cinnamon stick

Wash and dry the sour cherries and remove the stems. Mix with the sugar, red wine. and cinnamon stick and let sit overnight. The next day, remove the cinnamon stick and slowly bring the mixture to a boil. Add the rum and fill the jars while still hot. Close tightly.

❭ Tip

Ice cream, pudding, and pastry cream are delicious accompaniments to sour cherries in wine.

Plums in Armagnac

1 cup white wine
2–3 cups Armagnac
   (such as green
   Veltliner or Riesling)
2 cups dried plums
   (without pits)
1¼ cups sugar
½ cinnamon stick
2 cloves

Pour the white wine over the plums and let them soak for 1–2 days at room temperature. Put the fruit, white wine, sugar, cinnamon stick, and cloves into the jars and fill with Armagnac, fully covering the plums. Close the jars and let sit in a warm place for about 3 weeks. Strain the Armagnac and add again to the plums. Close the jars tightly.

Dried fruits in apricot brandy

1½ cups dried fruit
   (apricots, plums, apple
   rings, pineapple)
½ cup raisins
4 teaspoons peeled
   almonds
2 cups water
¾ cup sugar
3 cups apricot brandy

Wash the dried fruits and raisins briefly in hot water and dry with a paper towel. Put into jars with the almonds and cover with a clean cloth.

Boil the sugar in water until it has completely dissolved. Pour the brew over the fruit and fill the jars with apricot brandy. Close tightly and let sit at least 4 weeks in a cool and dry place.

❭ Tip

The dried fruits in apricot brandy are wonderful paired with vanilla ice cream and whipped cream.

RUM POTS
a brief description

There are many different varieties of rum pots. Work starts around June, when the early fruits are available. Later, more fruit varieties are added. Only around December will you be able to fully enjoy your work; the rum fruits now have their full aroma and there is nothing to prevent you from tasting them. Here's how to make a rum pot:

You will need the rum pot itself. Appropriate containers are glazed earthenware, porcelain, or glass. The rum pot should have a matching lid. The size of the opening is also important: since the fruit always has to be covered by a half-inch of liquid, it needs to be weighed down. A plate works well, but it has to fit into the mouth of the pot.

Select firm, ripe fruit without damage or bad spots. After washing and drying the fruit, always remove the stems. It's up to you whether to remove the pits in stone fruits.

Mix the fruit with the sugar and let sit, covered, in a cool place. Superfine sugar is best because it dissolves quickly. As a rule of thumb, the amount of sugar equals half the weight of the fruit. One exception is strawberries, where the ratio is 1:1.

Some recipes need less sugar. If in doubt, stick to the above basic rule. Bright and dark fruits should be sugared separately to preserve their color. If possible, add more fruit to the rum pot every two weeks.

Use only good-quality rum with an alcohol content of at least 54 percent for adequate preservation. Avoid rum with a very high alcohol content, as it tends to overpower the taste of the fruit.

Every time you add fruit, add rum to the pot, making sure the fruit is always covered.

Store the rum pot with a tight-fitting lid in a cool, dark place. There is no need to stir, as the sugar, alcohol, and fruit flavors combine on their own. However, it's a good idea to check occasionally to be sure the fruit is completely covered with rum.

Following are some trusted recipes that may also lead to quicker results than the above classic method. In these cases, the rum pot should soak for at least 3 weeks. The rule is that the longer you wait, the better the rum pot—however, no more than six months.

Select what you like for the rum pot. The following chart gives an overview of seasonal fruit. Blueberries are not really suitable for rum pots, as they tend to become mushy. Raspberries, blackberries, and white and red currants rot rather quickly. Apples tend to have a tart taste, and rhubarb is sour. However, these fruits are often found in rum pots; its composition is really up to you.

MONTH	FRUIT	PROCESSING
June	Strawberries	hull
	Blueberries	remove stalks
	Cherries	remove stalks, perhaps remove pits
July	Sour cherries	remove stalks, don't remove pits
	Black currants	remove stems
	Gooseberries	remove flowers and stalks
	Apricots	cut in half and remove pits
	Mirabelle plums	with pits
	Peaches	remove skin, cut in half, and remove pits
August	Nectarines	cut in half and remove pits
	Cantaloupes	peel, remove pits, and cut into 1-inch cubes
September	Prunes	cut in half and remove pits
	Pears	peel, cut into quarters, remove stalks and flowers, cut into three more pieces
	Grapes *without pits if possible*	remove stems
Independent of season	Pineapple	peel and cut into cubes
	Limes	cut into slices
	Kiwis	peel, cut into slices or large pieces
	Papayas	peel, cut into slices or large pieces

Fruit for rum pots—many
varieties are available

Summer rum pot

Wash the peaches and blanch them for 3 minutes in a pot of boiling water. Remove them
and shock thoroughly with cold water.

Then cut in half, remove pits, cut into quarters, and remove the skin with a small
knife. Cut into slices and mix with 1¼ cups of sugar. Cover and let soak for 3–4 hours.
Wash the cherries and apricots, cut in half, remove pits, and mix with the remaining
sugar. Pile the sugared fruit into a container, add the cinnamon stick and sliced vanilla
bean. Add the rum so that the fruit is covered by about a finger's width and close the
container tightly. Let soak for at least 3 weeks before serving.

3¼ cups rum (54% ABV)
2 large peaches
1 cup cherries
1 cup apricots
2 cups sugar
½ cinnamon stick
½ vanilla bean

Exotic rum pot

1 cup white rum (54%
    ABV)
3 oranges
3 kiwis
1 small pomegranate
1¼ cups sugar
½ vanilla bean

Peel the oranges and kiwis and cut into slices. Cut the pomegranate and use a spoon to remove the edible seeds. Mix the prepared fruit with the sugar, add the sliced vanilla bean and cover with the white rum so that the fruit is covered about a finger's width. Close the container tightly and let soak for at least 3 weeks before serving.

❭ Tip

The seeds are the edible parts of pomegranates. If you don't want the intense color in your rum pot, skip the pomegranates. You can enrich this exotic rum pot recipe with fresh figs and small pieces of pineapple. If you like sweet rum pots, just add more sugar.

Nut rum pot

1 cup rum
¾ cup walnut halves
¾ cup sugar
1 star anise
1 cinnamon stick

Boil the sugar with the rum until it has dissolved completely. Meanwhile, put the walnut sections with the spices into a prepared jar. Fill with the slightly cooled sugar-rum mix, close tightly, and let soak at least a week before serving.

❭ Tip

The nut rum pot is outstanding with ice cream.

Exotic rum pot (left)
Nut rum pot (right)

Vegetables in alcohol

Pumpkin in white wine

Cut the pumpkin into quarters and remove the seeds with a spoon, cut out the pulp, and cut into small cubes. Boil the sugar with the water, white wine, peppercorns, cloves, mace, and pumpkin pieces until they are firm to the bite. Fill jars while still hot and close immediately.

1 cup white wine
1 cup water
1 pound pumpkin
½ cup sugar
4 cloves
2 peppercorns
1 small piece of mace

❯ Tip

Do not use pumpkins with a high starch content for this recipe.

Pumpkin in white wine—
an autumn composition

White wine onions

Peel the onions and garlic cloves, put into boiling water, and boil for about 10 minutes. Strain with a sieve, drain, and cool. Boil the white wine with the white wine vinegar, salt, sugar, bay leaves, peppercorns, and mustard seeds until the salt and sugar are dissolved. Strain the brew and cool. Wash the tarragon sprig, dab dry, and pluck the leaves.

Put the onions, garlic cloves, and tarragon leaves into prepared glass jars and cover with the brew. Close the jars and store in a cool place.

3¼ cups dry white wine
1¾ cup white wine
  vinegar
2¼ pounds small onions
2 garlic cloves
1 sprig tarragon
1 cup sugar
1 tablespoon salt
1 teaspoon white
  peppercorns
1 teaspoon mustard
  seeds
2 bay leaves
saltwater

Red wine onions

1¾ cup strong red wine
¾ cup red wine vinegar
1 pound small, firm red onions
1 tablespoon white peppercorns
1 teaspoon salt
4 cloves
2 small bay leaves
½ cinnamon stick

Peel and cut the onions by cutting off the stems and roots. Leave the onions whole.

Mix the red wine vinegar with the red vinegar, sugar, salt, peppercorns, cloves, bayleaves, and the halved cinnamon stick. Put the onions into the brew and simmer for about 15 minutes. Remove the pot from the stove and cool. Use a skimmer to remove the onions and put into prepared jars. Boil the brew again, season, and pour into the jars. Close immediately and let sit at least 2–3 weeks before consumption.

> ❱ Tip

These red wine onions are far up on our list of favorites.

Garlic in Veltliner

1 cup Veltliner (white wine)
½ cup vinegar
1 tablespoon oil per jar
10 garlic cloves
1 red bell pepper
1 yellow bell pepper
1 green bell pepper
¼ cup sugar
2 tablespoons salt
1 teaspoon mustard seeds
6 peppercorns
6 cloves
3 juniper berries
3 bay leaves
thyme to taste
tarragon to taste

Peel the garlic cloves, wash and clean bell peppers and cut into strips or cubes.

Boil the white wine with the vinegar, sugar, salt, mustard seeds, peppercorns, cloves, juniper berries, bay leaves, thyme, and tarragon. Place the garlic cloves and bell pepper strips or cubes into the brew, boil for 3 minutes, and leave covered overnight in a cool place. Briefly bring to a boil the following day and fill small jars while liquid is hot. Add 1 tablespoon of oil. Close tightly and let soak for at least 10 days.

> ❱ Tip

Garlic in Veltliner is an original side dish for snacks and cold buffets.

Red wine onions—great look and taste

Pickling in Salt

Vegetables in salt

Fennel with root vegetables

2 tablespoons salt
2 cups water
2¼ pounds fennel bulbs
1 cup mixed root
   vegetables
5 peppercorns

Clean the fennel bulb and cut lengthwise. Wash the root vegetables and cut into small cubes. Boil the vegetables with the peppercorns in saltwater for 5 minutes and place in jars. Close tightly and use soon.

Gherkins

4 teaspoons salt
4¼ cups water
5½ pounds mid-sized
   gerkins
5 radish slices
3 grape leaves
4 tarragon sprigs
4 dill sprigs
2 teaspoons white
   peppercorns

Pile the gherkins into a bowl, cover with cold water and leave overnight. Brush well and dab dry.

Clean the tarragon, dill, and grape leaves under running water and let drip off well.

Place the gherkins into the jars, alternating with the horseradish slices, tarragon, dill, grape leaves, and peppercorns. Mix the water with the salt and pour over the gherkins so they are completely covered. Close the jars well. Leave the gherkins in a cool place for at least 4 weeks and control occasionally. In case you see a whitish layer of yeast after a period of time you need to rinse the gherkins well and renew the brew.

> ❯ Tip

Cover the gherkin brew with neutral vegetable oil—this may help to avoid the formation of yeast or mold.

Pickled radish

2 tablespoons salt
2 cups water
3 tablespoons white wine
   vinegar or distilled
   malt vinegar
3⅓ cups white radish
¾ cup red beets
3 garlic cloves

Finely grate the radish and the red beets. Peel the garlic and cut into thin slices. Pile the radish, red beets, and garlic slices into prepared jars. Boil the water, salt, and vinegar and pour it into the jars. Close tightly and serve soon.

Soup seasoning

Wash and clean the vegetables, peel, and grate finely. Wash the herbs and chop finely. Mix the chopped vegetables with the herbs and add salt. Fill the prepared jars tightly and close tightly. Store in a cool place.

❱ Tip

Use only small jars, as you will be using only small quantities. Keep jars in the refrigerator once they have been opened. This soup seasoning is a great alternative to stock cubes and sauces. Use 1–3 teaspoons for every 4 cups of soup, as desired.

1¼ cups cups salt
1¼ cups carrots
¾ cup celery
¾ cup parsley root
¾ cup parsnip
2 leeks
5 leaves of lovage
1 bunch of parsley

Pickled radish (left)
Soup seasoning (right)

Fruits in salt

Salt lemons

4 teaspoons salt, divided
5 small lemons
1 lemon (to press out)
water

Wash the lemons in hot water and place in a jar. Cover with water and set in a cool place for 3 days. Remove the lemons (the water will not be used) and quarter them lengthwise. Put 1 teaspon salt onto each lemon and put the lemons into the jar. Press out the remaining lemon and add the juice with the remaining 3 teaspoons of salt to the jar. Fill with boiling water until the lemons are totally covered. Close the jar and let sit at room temperature for about 3 weeks.

❯ Tip

You can use the whole lemons, or pieces of them, or just the peel. This recipe goes well with fish and meat dishes.

Eggs in salt

Pickled eggs

Wash the eggs thoroughly and boil for about 10 minutes. Remove and tap their pointed and blunt ends on the table so the shell cracks, but do not peel. Peel the onions and cut into rings.

Briefly boil the water with the apple vinegar, salt, onions, thyme, rosemary, dill umbel, peppercorns, and mustard seeds. Put the eggs with their shell into a large jar and pour the brew over them once it has cooled a bit. The herbs should be spread throughout the glass. Refrigerate for a week before serving.

⟩ Tip

Pickled eggs are usually seasoned before eating. You can use pepper, vinegar, oil, salt, and many different sauces.

⅓ cup salt
5⅓ cups water
3 tablespoons apple
   vinegar
12 eggs
2 small red onions
1 bay leaf
1 sprig thyme
1 sprig rosemary
1 dill umbel
a few peppercorns
½ teaspoon mustard
   seeds
saltwater to boil the eggs

Preparing pickled eggs

Hardboil the eggs (if they come from the fridge, dip briefly three times in boiling water so that the shell does not crack).

Shock the eggs with cold water and tap them on a hard surface so the shell cracks and the brew can be absorbed.

A spicy potpourri—colorful peppercorns, mustard seeds, dill, thyme, rosemary, and onion.

Briefly boil water with apple cider vinegar, salt, and spices.

Put the eggs with their shells into a glass jar and pour the cooled brew over them. The glass should be placed onto a moist surface. Make sure the spices mix thoroughly. Close the jar tightly.

Fish in salt

Pickled anchovies

Rub some of the fine sea salt into the anchovies' cavity and outer skin. Layer the anchovies in a broad, flat bowl. Pour the rest of the sea salt over each layer. Cover and marinate in the refrigerator for 4–5 hours until the juices are released. Remove the fish and pat dry with a paper towel.

Put some of the coarse sea salt into the bottom of a prepared large jar. Layer the fish with one bay leaf, a few peppercorns, and a thin layer of coarse salt, topping off with another layer of coarse salt. Place a plate on top of the fish and add weight with a bottle filled with water. Marinate in the refrigerator for about a week before serving. The pickled anchovies should be consumed soon.

6⅓ cups coarse salt
2 cups fine sea salt
2¼ pounds anchovies (eviscerated and cleaned)
1 tablespoon black peppercorns
4 bay leaves

❭ Tip

Make sure you use only young, fresh fish of about the same size, with undamaged, shiny skin. Before serving, soak the anchovies in cold water for about 15 minutes to curb the intense saltiness.

PICKLED

Vinegar, Oil, and Alcohol

Delicacies

Pickling in Vinegar

Fruits in vinegar

Apples in lemon balm vinegar

1¾ cup apple cider vinegar
¾ cup apple juice
¾ cup water
2¼ pounds small, sour apples
¾ cup cane sugar
juice and peel of 1 lemon
4 sprigs lemon balm
lemon water (juice of 1 lemon per 1 quart of water)

Wash the apples, peel (save peels for later), and remove the core. Put them in lemon water to keep them from turning brown. Wash the lemon balm under cold running water and dab dry. Boil the apple peels, lemon peel, and lemon balm leaves for 10 minutes. Strain and boil again with the apple cider vinegar, apple juice, and cane sugar. Steam the apples in this brew until they are somewhat soft, remove with a skimmer, and put into the prepared jars. Boil the brew once again and pour over the apples. Close while still hot and store in a cool place.

❯ Tip

Halved or sliced, these apples are a great side dish for roasted meat.

Ginger apples

1½ cup vinegar
1½ cup water
3⅓ pounds sour apples
juice and peel of 1 lemon
1¾ cup sugar
½ teaspoon ground ginger
5 cloves
1 cinnamon stick

Wash the lemon with hot water, peel thinly, and press out the juice. Wash the apples, peel and remove the core. Immediately sprinkle with lemon juice to keep it from turning brown. Boil the vinegar, water, sugar, cinnamon stick, cloves, lemon peel, and ginger. Steam the apples for about 10 minutes. Remove with a skimmer and put into jars. Pour the brew over the apples and close tightly. Store in a cool place and consume soon.

❯ Tip

Vary the amount of sugar depending on the apple variety and your personal taste.

Ginger apples (left) and Spice pears (right)

Spiced pears

Make lemon water by adding lemon juice to a large bowl of water. Peel a few lengthwise strips from each pear and put them into the lemon water.

Boil the red wine with the red wine vinegar, sugar, honey, and spice bag (consisting of peppercorns, cloves, bay leaves, cinnamon sticks, and lemon peel) and simmer for 5 minutes. Put the pears into the brew and simmer for 35–40 minutes until they are softer but offer resistance when pricked. Remove with a skimmer and put into the jar. Simmer the brew until its volume is reduced by half, and remove the spice bag. Pour the brew over the pears so they are completely covered. Close tightly and let soak for 1 month before serving.

4¼ cups red wine vinegar
2 cups red wine
2¼ pounds small, hard pears
juice of 1 lemon
a few strips of lemon peel
1¾ cup sugar
½ cup honey
1 tablespoon black peppercorns
2 teaspoons cloves
2 teaspoons allspice berries
2 bay leaves
2 cinnamon sticks

Pears in vinegar sugar

Cut the peeled and cored pears into even strips. Boil the apple cider vinegar with the water, rock sugar, cloves, cinnamon stick, and lemon peel. Put the fruit into the brew and boil until the fruit is somewhat soft. Remove with the skimmer and put into jars. Boil the brew once again and pour over the fruit. Close tightly and store in a cool place.

1½ cup apple cider vinegar
1½ cup water
3⅓ pounds pears
1¾ cup rock sugar
5 cloves
1 cinnamon stick
peel of 1 lemon

Curry pears

Halve the peeled pears and remove the core. Immediately pour some wine vinegar over them to keep them from getting brown. Boil the remaining wine vinegar, white wine, orange and lemon juices, and sugar. Put the pear halves into the brew and boil until soft. Remove with a skimmer and drain. Grind the allspice and cilantro finely, mix with the curry and cardamom, and add to the brew. Boil until the syrup is slightly thick.

Pile the pear halves into jars and pour the strained, cooled syrup over them. Close tightly and store in a cool, dry place. Let soak for about 2 months before serving.

4¼ cups wine vinegar
2 cups light, soft white wine
4½ pounds small, firm pears
4 cups sugar
juice and peel of ½ an orange
juice and peel of ½ a lemon
2 tablespoons curry powder
1½ teaspoons allspice berries
½ teaspoon cilantro
1 pinch of cardamom

Vinegar pears

1½ cups wine vinegar
1½ cups water
2¼ pounds firm pears
1¾ cups sugar
1 cinnamon stick
5 cloves

Peel, core, and halve the pears.

Boil the water, sugar, wine vinegar, cinnamon stick, and cloves for the brew. Add the pear halves and continue boiliing for about 5 minutes. Remove the pears and put into jars. Pour the boiling liquid over them and close tightly.

Sweet and sour pears in cider

¾ cup pear or apple cider
   vinegar
¾ cup cider
2¼ pounds cider pears
 2 small shots pear
   brandy
1 cup sugar
½ cup brown rock sugar
1 teaspoon mustard
   seeds
1 teaspoon juniper
   berries
4 cloves
1 sprig thyme
½ sprig marjoram
1 bay leaf
1 cinnamon stick

Thoroughly wash the pears, but do not remove the stems or peel. Prick the fruit a few times. Boil the vinegar with the cider, sugar, rock sugar, mustard seeds, juniper berries, thyme, rosemary, bay leaf, cinnamon stick, and cloves. Put the pears into the brew and steam until they are al dente. Remove the pears with a skimmer and close the jars tightly. Boil the brew again and add the pear brandy. Pour the boiling brew through a sieve into the jars. Put the strained spices (without the thyme and rosemary) into the jars so they look appealing. Close tightly immediately and store in a cool, dark place. Let soak for about 1 month before serving.

> **❱ Tip**

Sweet and sour cider pears are an unusual and attractive side dish for beef and venison roasts, cheese, and pies.

Gooseberries with a shot

½ cup red wine vinegar
½ cup strong,
   dry red wine
½ cup Armagnac
3¼ cups gooseberries
1½ cups sugar
1 cinnamon stick

Wash the gooseberries, dab dry and put into the jars. Boil the red wine, red wine vinegar, sugar, and cinnamon stick. As soon as the sugar has dissolved, remove frorm the stove and let cool down. Pour the brew over the berries and evenly distribute the armagnac among the jars. Close tightly.

Spicy elderberries

Slowly boil the wine vinegar with the rock sugar, ginger, radish, peppercorns, allspice corns, cloves, cinnamon stick, and mace for 10 minutes. Strain and simmer the elderberries for 5 minutes in the brew. Fill the jars and close tightly while still hot. Consume soon.

❱ Tip

The spicy elderberries are great as a side dish for pies, roast beef, and meats in gelatin.

2 cups wine vinegar
2¼ pounds elderberries
1¾ cups rock sugar
⅓-inch ginger
1 tablespoon grated
   radish
5 black peppercorns
3 allspice berries
5 cloves
1 cinnamon stick
1 teaspoon mace

Figs in cardamom syrup

Thoroughly wash the figs, cut in half, and remove the stem. Use a small knife to zest the orange peel. Combine the orange zest, sugar, cardamom powder, cinnamon stick, white wine vinegar, and water, and boil for about 5 minutes. Put the figs into the jars and cover with the hot brew. Close tightly and store in the refrigerator.

❱ Tip

Figs in cardamom syrup is one of our favorite recipes. Serve this delicacy as an antipasto, with cold meats, or with ham. Stored in the refrigerator, the figs will last for about 1 month. Consume them within the first two weeks for optimal appearance and consistency.

¾ cup white wine vinegar
1¾ cups water
10 fresh, ripe figs
1 orange
1 cup sugar
¼ teaspoon cardamom
   powder
1 cinnamon stick

Figs in cardamom syrup (left)
Spicy elderberries (right)

Sweet and sour apricots

½ cup white wine vinegar
2 cups water
3½ pounds apricots
⅓-inch fresh ginger root
1¾ cup sugar
3 tablespoons elderberry syrup
1 vanilla bean

Halve the apricots and remove the pits. Peel the ginger, cut into thin slices, and cut the vanilla bean into small pieces. Boil the white wine vinegar with water, sugar, ginger slices, syrup, and vanilla pieces. Briefly boil the apricots in this brew. Remove with a skimmer and pile into jars. Reduce the brew, uncovered, at high heat for 15 minutes, then pour over the apricots while still hot. Close tightly and store in a cool, dry place. Serve within two weeks.

Dutch cherries

2 cups mild wine vinegar
1 cup currant juice
⅓ ounce kirsch
4½ pounds firm black cherries
4 cups white rock sugar
1 cinnamon stick
2 juniper berries

Wash the cherries and remove the stems and pits. The fruits should not be damaged. Heat the wine vinegar with the currant juice, cinnamon stick, and juniper berries, and pour over the cherries while still warm. Store covered in the refrigerator for about 2 days and shake thoroughly now and then.

Strain the brew, add the coarsely crushed rock sugar, and heat it until it is dissolved. Briefly boil the cherries in the brew and remove with a skimmer. Allow the brew to reduce into a light syrup. Use the kirsch to rinse a jar. Fill the jar with the cherries, taking out the juniper berries and the cinnamon stick. Pour the syrup over them, close tightly, and store in a cool place for at least 2 months.

Sweet and sour apricots (left)
Dutch cherries (right)

Vinegar cherries

Wash the cherries and remove the stems and pits, catching the juice in a bowl.
Mix the cherry juice with the red wine vinegar and sugar. Boil for 10 minutes and cool.
Crush half the mustard seeds, leave the rest intact, and put all of them into a jar with
the cherries. Pour in the cold brew and close the jar. Store in a cool place for at least 14
days before serving.

½ cup red wine vinegar
1 pound cherries
1 cup sugar
1 teaspoon mustard
  seeds

Old British-style currants

Wash the currants, remove the stems, dab dry, and place in a jar. Boil the sugar, water,
and wine vinegar. Make a spice bag with the spice ingredients and add it to the pot.
Simmer for 15 minutes on medium heat, stirring occasionally. Remove the spice bag and
let the brew cool. Pour over the berries. Close the jar and let soak for at least 4 weeks.

> ❱ Tip

Mix white currants with the red and black currants for an appealing look. Old British-style
currants make a good garnish for red cabbage.

2½ cups wine vinegar
½ cup water
2¼ pounds red currants
1 pound black currants
1 cup brown sugar
1 small piece of dried
  ginger (or ginger
  powder)
5 black peppercorns
3 coriander seeds
2 cloves
1 piece of mace
¼ cinnamon stick
3 teaspoons grated
  radish

Currants Old British-
style—an alternative
to cranberries for spicy
dishes

Kiwi bell pepper pickles

1 cup apple vinegar or
white wine vinegar
7 firm, unripe kiwis
1 small red bell pepper
juice of ¼ lemon
2½ tablespoons blossom
honey
¼ cup sugar
½ tablespoons salt
5 black peppercorns
3 juniper berries
4 allspice berries

Peel the kiwis and cut into thick slices. Wash the bell pepper and cut into broad strips. In a bowl, sprinkle lemon juice over the kiwi slices and let sit for 15 minutes. In another bowl, sprinkle the salt over the bell pepper strips and let sit for 15 minutes.

Mix together the vinegar, honey, sugar, peppercorns, juniper berries, and allspice berries. Boil for 10 minutes at high heat to reduce the liquid. Rinse the bell pepper strips with cold water, drain, and add to the liquid, simmering for 5 minutes. Add the kiwis and simmer for another 5 minutes.

Remove the kiwi slices and bell pepper strips with a skimmer and add to the jars. Boil the brew for another 10 minutes until it is further reduced. Fill the jars with the boiling hot mixture. Close tightly and let soak for a few days.

Pepper melons

¾ cup fruit vinegar
¼ cup water
2¼ pounds honeydew
melon
2 cups sugar
1 tablespoon ginger
½ teaspoon white
peppercorns
¼ teaspoon cayenne
pepper
3 cloves
1 pinch of nutmeg

Slice the honeydew melon lengthwise. Use a spoon to remove the pits and soft, watery pulp—only the firm fruit pulp should remain. Remove the pulp from the peel and cut into bite-sized pieces. Peel the ginger root and cut into very fine slices. Put the melon pieces and the ginger slices into a bowl. Mix the sugar with the peppercorns, cayenne pepper, and nutmeg and add to the bowl with the fruit. Mix thoroughly, cover, and leave overnight in a cool place.

The next day, let the fruit drain into a sieve—catch the juice. Mix the fruit juice with the fruit vinegar, water, and cloves and bring to a boil. Add the fruit and boil until it becomes glassy. Remove with a skimmer and fill the glasses. Boil the brew again until it reaches a syrupy consistency. Skim, if necessary. Fill the jars with the hot liquid and close tightly immediately. Store in a cool, dry, dark place.

Sweet and sour chunky melon (left)
Pepper melon (right)

Sweet and sour chunky melon

Cut the melons in half lengthwise, remove the seeds and soft inner pulp with a spoon. Cut each half into 4–5 slices, and then halve the slices. Peel and slice the ginger. Boil the white wine, vinegar essence, honey, ginger slices, star anise, and cloves for about 10 minutes. Soak the lemon slices in the brew for 5 minutes. Remove with a skimmer and drain. Pile the lemon slices into jars and pour the hot brew over them. Close immediately and store in a cool place.

8–9 tablespoons vinegar essence (25%)
2 cups white wine
1 cup water
6⅓ cups pineapple melon
1¼ cups honey
1 tablespoon fresh ginger root
3 star anise
3 cloves

Christmas oranges

Wash the oranges thoroughly and cut into ¾-inch-thick slices. Press the cloves into the orange peel. Boil the orange slices with the water, lemon juice, and spice bag (cloves, cardamom pods, cinnamon stick) and simmer for 5 minutes.

Meanwhile, prepare a brew with the apple cider vinegar, water, sugar, and lemon peel, and boil for about 10 minutes. Pile the orange slices into jars. Boil the brew once again, pour into the jars while still hot, and close tightly.

1 cup apple cider vinegar
1 cup water
1 pound thin-skinned seedless oranges
¾ cup sugar
peel and juice of 1 lemon
cloves
2 cloves
1 small crushed cinnamon stick
3 crushed cardamom pods

Vegetables in vinegar

Eggplant with red beets

¾ cup apple cider vinegar
2¼ pounds baby eggplant
1 cup red beets
5 garlic cloves
2 fresh red chilli peppers
2 teaspons salt
2 cups water

Trim the eggplant and steam for 5–8 minutes. It should not be too soft. Peel and coarsely chop the garlic cloves. Peel the beets and grate finely. Coarsely chop the chilli peppers.

Put the eggplant and remaining ingredients into the prepared jars. Boil the apple cider vinegar and water with salt, and pour over the vegetables. Place wooden spatula pieces on top to keep the vegetables submerged, and close the jars. Store in a cool place for a week and consume soon.

❱ Tip

If you are using normal-sized eggplant, cut it into quarters.

Eggplant with white wine vinegar

½ to ¾ cup white wine
      vinegar
1 pound eggplant
6 garlic cloves
1¼ cup water
½ cup honey
1 dried chilli pod

Cut the eggplant in half lengthwise and into ⅓-inch discs. Peel the garlic. Boil the vinegar, honey, water, and chili pods for 5 minutes. Then add the eggplant and garlic and boil for another 3 minutes. Remove the chili pod. Put the eggplant and garlic into the prepared jars and fill with the hot brew. Enjoy this delicacy within 2 weeks.

Gherkins with shallots

4¼ cups white wine
      vinegar
4¼ cups water
3⅓ pounds small
      cucumbers
3 tablespoons salt
12 shallots
5 sprigs dill
2 teaspoons colored
      peppercorns
3 teaspoons mustard
      seeds
2 small bay leaves

Wash the cucumbers under running water with a brush and remove the stems. Put into a bowl, add salt and water, and let soak for 24 hours.

Remove the cucumbers from the liquid and rinse with cold water. Peel the shallots and cut into rings. Coarsely chop the dill. Fill the jars tightly with the cucumbers, shallots, bay leaves, peppercorns, and mustard seeds. Boil the white wine vinegar and fill the jars. Close tightly and let soak at least 2 weeks.

❱ Tip

For extended shelf life, sterilize the cucumbers and shallots in a water bath for 30 minutes.

Spicy-hot gherkins

Wash the gherkins with a brush under running water and remove the stems. Put into a bowl and sprinkle with sea salt, add 6 cups of water, stir, and let soak for 24 hours.

Remove the gherkins from the brew and rinse with cold water.

Peel and slice the radish. Wash the chilli pods, remove the seeds, and cut into rings. Coarsely chop the dill. Boil the apple vinegar with 2 cups of water, sea salt, sugar, peppercorns, juniper berries, bay leaf, and dill. Pile the gherkins into jars and cover with the hot brew. Close tightly and store at least two weeks.

❱ Tip

Once the jar has been opened, remove the gherkins only with clean utensils, such as decorative wooden tongs.

2 cups apple cider
   vinegar
8 cups water
2¼ pounds gerkins
2½ tablespoons radish
3 small chilli pods
3 sprigs dill
½ cup sea salt
½ cup sugar
1 tablespoon salt
2 tablespoons colored
   peppercorns
1 tablespoon juniper
   berries
1 bay leaf

Eggplant in white wine vinegar (left) and Gherkins with shallots (right)

Sour gherkins

3 cups wine vinegar

1 cup water

3½ pounds small, firm gerkins

3 tablespoons salt

2 teaspoons colored peppercorns

1 teaspoon sugar

salt to taste

optional: shallots, dill, mustard seeds, sliced radish, grape leaves

Wash the gherkins with a brush under running water and remove the stems. Put into a bowl and sprinkle with 3 tablespoons salt, add 4 cups water, and let soak for a few hours. Remove the gherkins from the liquid and rinse. Prick the gherkins with a thick needle and place into jars. Add a few grape leaves, peeled shallots, dill umbels, mustard seeds, and a few slices of fresh radish if you wish.

Boil the wine vinegar with 1 cup water, peppercorns, sugar, and salt. Cool and pour into the jars. Close tightly and store in a cool, dark place.

Sweet and sour gherkins

3 cups wine vinegar

1¼ cups water

3⅓ pounds small, firm cucumbers

3 tablespoons salt

3 tablespoons sugar

¾-inch cinnamon stick

6 cloves

salt as desired

1 sprig dill

1 tablespoon mustard seeds

Wash the gherkins with a brush under running water and remove the stems. Place into a bowl and sprinkle with 3 tablespoons salt. Add 4 cups of water, mix, and let soak for a few hours. Remove the vegetables from the brew and rinse. Prick with a thick needle and place with the dill and mustard seeds into the jars.

Combine the wine vinegar, water, sugar, cinnamon stick, cloves, and salt, and boil for a few minutes. Cool down and strain into the jars. Close tightly and store in a dark place.

> ❱ Tip

If you discover that the vinegar has become turbid, strain it again, boil, and fill the jars once more.

Spicy dill

2 cups apple cider vinegar

4 cups water

6½ pounds small cucumbers

4 onions

4 bell peppers

2 carrots

½ cup sugar

salt to taste

1 package pickling spices

Peel the cucumbers, remove the seeds, and cut in a petal fashion. Cut the onions and bell peppers into rings and slice the carrots. Mix together in a bowl, add salt, and let soak for 3 hours. Boil the apple cider vinegar with the water, sugar, and spices, stirring. Add the vegetables and boil briefly. Fill the jars while still hot.

Sweet and sour cucumbers with pearl onions

Brush the cucumbers under cold running water. Peel the onions. Steam the cucumbers and onions in saltwater for 2 minutes, remove and drain.

Boil the vinegar with the sugar, salt, mustard seeds, peppercorns, and chilli peppers for 5 minutes.

Rinse the tarragon and pat dry.

Put the cucumbers, onions, and tarragon into the prepared jars and pour the boiling liquid over them. Close the jars immediately and store in a cool place.

3¼ cups vinegar
3½ pounds very small pickling cucumbers
1¼ cups pearl onions
1 chili pepper
4 sprigs tarragon
2 cups fine sugar
½ cup salt
1 tablespoon mustard seeds
1 tablespoon peppercorns
saltwater for blanching

Mustard cucumber pickle

Peel the cucumbers, remove the stems, cut in half lengthwise, and scrape out the seeds with a spoon. Cut the cucumber pulp into 1-inch-thick pieces, sprinkle with 1 tablespoon salt, and soak overnight in a covered bowl.

Heat the water with the white wine vinegar, remaining salt, sugar, mustard seeds, and bay leaves until the sugar has dissolved. Strain the brew and put aside the spices and liquid to use later.

Peel the onions and cut into rings. Peel and slice the radish. Boil the brew, add the drained cucumber pieces one by one, boil briefly, and remove with a skimmer.

Fill the jars with the cucumber pieces, alternating with the radish, onion rings, and spices. Add the brew until the cucumbers are covered with a half-inch of liquid. Close tightly and store in a cool place for at least 3 weeks.

6⅓ cups white wine vinegar
2 cups water
5½ pounds firm, yellow-white cucumbers
1¼ cups onions
3 tablespoons radish
1½ cups sugar
2 tablespoons salt
1 tablespoons mustard seeds
3 small bay leaves

Sweet and sour cucumbers with pearl onions (left)
Mustard cucumbers (right)

Colorful vegetables

1½ cups white wine
    vinegar
3¼ cups water
2¼ pounds cucumbers
1¾ cups onions
1¼ cups carrots
4 garlic cloves
4 tablespoons sugar
2 teaspoons salt
1 tablespoon black
    peppercorns
3–4 bay leaves

Cut the cucumbers into ⅓-inch slices. Peel the onions and cut into thin rings. Julienne or coarsely grate the carrots. Slice the garlic. In a sieve, mix the cucumber slices with 1 tablespoon salt and soak for 20 minutes. Rinse under cold running water and drain.

Pour boiling water into a bowl with the onion rings and the julienne carrots, and drain well. Put a layer of cucumber slices into the jar, add a few garlic cloves, peppercorns, and 1 bay leaf and cover with the onions and carrots. Repeat until the jar is filled to the rim, layering loosely. Combine water, vinegar, sugar, and remaining salt and boil for a few minutes at medium heat. Pour the hot vinegar mix over the vegetables to cover. Close tightly and store in the refrigerator for at least 2 days.

Colorful vegetables —a refreshing side dish with a delicate, sour taste

Corn cobs in vinegar

Combine the corn cobs and salt and store in the refrigerator for 24 hours. Pat the corn cobs dry and place vertically into the jars. Add the peppercorns, basil, and radish. Boil the white wine vinegar, pour over the corncobs, and close the jars tightly.

2 cups white wine vinegar
4 cups baby corn cobs
3 sprigs tarragon
1 tablespoon salt
1 teaspoon colored
    peppercorns
1 teaspoon basil
1 teaspoon grated radish

Pickled garlic

Peel the garlic cloves and cut the peppers into thin rings.

In a saucepan, combine the wine vinegar, salt, sugar, thyme, rosemary, and peppercorns. Add the garlic cloves and peppers and boil for 10 minutes. Pour into the jars while still hot and cover with the olive oil. Close tightly and store in a cool place.

¾ cup wine vinegar
about ¼ cup olive oil
1¼ cups garlic
2 mild peppers
4 teaspoons sugar
1 tablespoon salt
1 sprig dried thyme
3–5 rosemary needles
5–8 colored peppercorns,
    to taste

Pickled garlic—healthy with a mild taste

Spicy garlic

Peel the garlic. Combine the herb vinegar, water, oil, mustard, mustard seeds, sugar, salt, and garlic, and boil for about 3 minutes. Pour the hot mixture into the jars and close tightly.

1 cup herb vinegar
1 cup water
splash of oil
2 cups garlic cloves
1½ teaspoons mustard
    seeds
1½ teaspoons sugar
1 tablespoon salt
1½ teaspoons spicy-hot
    mustard

Pickled green asparagus

2¼ pounds green
   asparagus
½ teaspoon sugar
1 tablespoon butter
1¾ cup white wine
   vinegar
½ cup water
1 teaspoon sugar
1 sprig tarragon
1 sprig thyme
5 black peppercorns
½ cup canola oil

Wash the asparagus, pat dry, and remove the tough ends. Use strings to tie it into bundles and immerse in boiling saltwater with the sugar and butter. Boil the asparagus for about 10 minutes (depending on its thickness), drain, and remove the strings. Boil the white wine vinegar, water, sugar, herbs, peppercorns, and canola oil. Pack the asparagus tightly into a tall jar, pour the hot marinade over it, close tightly, and store in the refrigerator for two days. Serve soon.

❱ Tip

Use tall jars to hold the upright asparagus, or cut the asparagus to the jar height (the rest can be used for asparagus soup). Enjoy the pickled asparagus as an appetizer with prosciutto or cream cheese and bread.

Mildly spicy pickled green asparagus (left) and Pickled green asparagus (right)

Mildly spicy pickled green asparagus

Wash the asparagus and pat dry. Peel from the head toward the end, and cut off the tough ends. Tie the asparagus with string and place in boiling saltwater with the sugar and butter. Cover and boil the asparagus for about 15 minutes (depending on thickness). Drain and remove the strings. Pack the asparagus tightly into a tall glass and add the piri piri. Wash the lemon and peel thinly. Boil the lemon with the water, spices, and lemon peel, pour the hot liquid over the asparagus, and close tightly. Allow to sit for 2–3 weeks before serving.

❯ Tip

Use tall jars to hold the upright asparagus, or cut the asparagus to the height of the jars (the rest can be used for asparagus soup).

2¼ pounds white
  asparagus
saltwater
½ teaspoon sugar
½ cup butter
1 cup white wine vinegar
1 cup water
1 lemon
1 bay leaf
5 black peppercorns
1 teaspoon sugar
1 piri piri per jar

Pickled asparagus

Wash the asparagus (do not peel green asparagus), removing the tough ends if necessary. Boil with the lemon slices for about 8 minutes (1 teaspoon salt per 4 cups water) and let cool in the saltwater.

Measure 3 cups of the saltwater and add the white wine vinegar, sugar, and peppercorns, and boil for about 5 minutes. Add salt to this brew if desired.

Put the asparagus upright into tall jars, add the tarragon between the asparagus spears, and pour the boiling brew over it. Close tightly.

❯ Tip

When an asparagus spear bends slightly when placed over a fork, it is perfectly cooked.

1 cup white wine vinegar
2¼ pounds green
  asparagus
2 slices lemon
3 tablespoons sugar
10 white peppercorns
salt
2 sprigs fresh tarragon

Sweet and sour radish

Peel the radishes and cut into ¼-inch slices. Boil the apple cider vinegar with the sugar, peppercorns, nutmeg, and mustard seeds. Add the radish slices and steam until they are glassy. Then remove them and boil the liquid for about 10 minutes to reduce the volume. Pile the radish slices into the jars and cover with the hot brew. Close tightly and store in a cool place.

2 cups apple cider
  vinegar
2¼ pounds radish
3¼ cups sugar
½ teaspoon peppercorns
½ teaspoon nutmeg
1 tablespoon mustard
  seeds

Sweet and sour carrots

3 cups apple cider
   vinegar
3 cups clear apple juice
1 teaspon olive oil
2¼ pounds same-sized
   carrots
1 piece of leek
1 garlic clove
1 cup sugar
1 bay leaf
1 teaspoon salt
2 star anise
2 cloves
5 allspice berries
½ teaspoon curry powder
1½ teaspoons fennel or
   aniseed

Peel and quarter the carrots lengthwise. Clean the leek and cut the same way. Peel and quarter the garlic clove. Heat the oil in a large, wide pot and add the garlic and bay leaf, stirring until they give off an aroma. Add the apple cider vinegar, apple juice, sugar, salt, star anise, cloves, allspice berries, curry powder, and the fennel or aniseed, and bring to a boil.

Steam the carrots in this brew at low heat for 15–20 minutes, until al dente. Add the leek about 5 minutes before finishing. Remove from the heat, cover, and let sit in a cool place for 3 days.

Remove the carrots and the leek from the brew and cut so that they fit upright in the jars. Boil the brew again and pour it into the jars, completely covering the vegetables. Close tightly and store in a cool, dark place. Let soak at least 2 weeks before serving.

Carrot salad

1¾ cup fruit vinegar
1¾ cup water
2¼ pounds carrots
1 sour apple
1 large onion
juice of ½ lemon
4 tablespoons sugar
1½ teaspoons salt
1½ teaspoons colored
   peppercorns
½ teaspoon mustard
   seeds
½ teaspoon anise
1 bay leaf
1 pinch of mustard
   powder
saltwater

Peel and core the apple and cut into quarters. Finely grate the carrots and apples and toss with the lemon juice. Blanch the carrot-apple mix for about 3 minutes in saltwater. Empty the mix into a sieve and drain thoroughly, then pack into the jars.

Peel the onions, cut into large pieces, and vigorously boil for about 8 minutes with the fruit vinegar, water, sugar, salt, peppercorns, mustard seeds, aniseed, bay leaf, and mustard powder. Strain the hot brew and pour it into the jars. Close tightly and let cool. Serve soon.

Sweet and sour carrots—
these sweet-spicy-hot
carrots taste great.

Carrot-celery mix

Cut the celery and carrots into thin slices or grate coarsely. Peel the onions and cut into thin rings. Mix the celery, carrots, onions, and salt thoroughly and let soak for about 2 hours. Press and mix with your hands. Add the dill and orange peel to the vegetable mix and pile loosely into jars.

Boil the vinegar, water, sugar, and orange juice and let sit for several minutes, then skim off any residue. Pour the brew into the jars, close tightly, and let soak for a week before serving.

2 cups white wine or apple vinegar
¾ cup water
1 tablespoon sugar
juice of 1 orange
7 large celery stalks
5 large carrots
2 onions
salt as desired
2 tablespoon dill
peel of an orange, cut into strips

Spiced pumpkin

Coarsely chop the garlic. Remove the seeds from the chili peppers and cut into thin rings. Mix together the red wine vinegar, garlic, chili peppers, sugar, peppercorns, cloves, and bay leaf, and boil until the sugar is dissolved.

Cut the pumpkin into 1-inch cubes and steam in the brew for 4–5 minutes. Remove with a skimmer, drain, and fill the jars. Pour the hot liquid over the pumpkin until it is completely covered. Close and store in a cool place.

2 cups red wine vinegar
1⅓ pounds raw pumpkin (weigh after cleaning)
2 dried, red chili peppers
1 garlic clove
1 cup sugar
1 teaspoon black peppercorns
2 cloves
1 bay leaf

Carrot-celery mix (left) Spiced pumpkin (right)

Pumpkin with ginger

1 cup wine vinegar
½ cup water
2¼ pounds raw pumpkin
2 cups sugar
1 tablespoon fresh ginger
   root
½ teaspoon turmeric

Remove the pumpkin seeds and cut into even-sized pieces. Peel the ginger root and cut into thin slices. Mix the pumpkin and ginger pieces. Bring the wine vinegar, water, and turmeric to a boil and pour over the pumpkin-ginger mixture. Cover and let sit for 24 hours. Strain the vinegar water, add the sugar, and bring to a boil until the pumpkin becomes translucent. Put the pumpkin pieces and ginger into jars and cover with the hot brew. Close tightly and serve soon.

Pumpkin with oranges

¼ cup wine vinegar
3¼ cups water, divided
2¼ pounds raw pumpkin
juice and zest of 2
   oranges
½ cup sugar
3 cloves
1 cinnamon stick

Peel the pumpkin, remove the seeds and pulp with a spoon, and cut into medium-sized strips. Dilute the wine vinegar with ½ cup of water, pour over the pumpkin strips, and let soak for 24 hours.

Remove the pumpkin strips with a skimmer and drain. Bring the remaining water to a boil and add the pumpkin, sugar, cinnamon, cloves, and orange zest. When the pumpkin is soft, add the orange juice and fill the jars. Close tightly, store in the fridge, and serve soon.

Sweet and sour pumpkin

1 cup white wine vinegar
1 cup water
2¼ pounds pumpkin
½ lemon, cut into slices
1 cup sugar
4 allspice berries
4 cloves
1 teaspoon mustard
   seeds
1 cinnamon stick

Peel the pumpkin, remove the seeds and pulp with a spoon, and cut into even-sized pieces. Boil the white wine vinegar with the water, sugar, allspice berries, cloves, mustard seeds, and cinnamon stick. Steam the pumpkin pieces in this brew until translucent. Drain, spoon into jars, and add the orange peel. Cover with the hot liquid, close tightly, and serve soon.

Red beets

Peel the red beets and cut into thin slices. Peel and core the apples and cut into cubes. Peel the onion and cut into thin rings. Pile the red beets, apple pieces, and onion rings into a jar, alternating with the peppercorns, cloves, and bay leaves. Boil the wine vinegar, water, radish, sugar, salt, and caraway, and pour over the beets. Close tightly and store in a cool place.

> ❱ Tip

Enjoy the red beets right away or store them for an extended period.

1 cup wine vinegar
¼ cup water
1 slice of radish
sugar and salt to taste
1 teaspoon caraway
2¼ pounds boiled red
    beets
1 large apple
1 large onion
12 peppercorns
6 cloves
2 small bay leaves

Sweet and sour bell pepper

Wash the bell peppers, cut in half, remove seeds and blanch in boiling water for a few minutes. Peel the onions and garlic cloves, cut in half and pile with bell pepper halves into jars. Boil the white wine vinegar with the sugar, salt, peppercorns, and bay leaves and pour over the vegetables while still boiling hot. Close immediately, let cool down and store in a cool place.

3¼ cups white wine
    vinegar
2¼ pounds red, green,
    and yellow bell
    peppers
3 small onions
3 garlic cloves
¾ cup sugar
1 teaspoon salt
1 teaspoon white
    peppercorns
3 bay leaves

Sweet and sour bell peppers—an eyecatching condiment.

Tomato-onion pot

1¾ cups herb vinegar

2 cups sugar

3⅓ pounds small,
    firm tomatoes

1 pound small onions

1 sprig tarragon

1 teaspoon salt

1 teaspoon black
    peppercorns

Wash the tomatoes, remove the stems, and prick several times. Combine the peeled onions with the tomatoes and herb vinegar in a bowl and store in a cool place overnight.

The next day, strain the vinegar and boil with the onions, sugar, salt, and peppercorns. When the onions are tender, remove them and set aside. Pile the tomatoes, onions, and tarragon into the prepared jars. Reduce the vinegar mix to a thin syrup and fill the jars. Close tightly and store in a cool place until ready to serve.

Pickled celery

4¼ cups lemon vinegar

2 cups water

4½ pounds small celery
    bulbs

3 onions

½ bunch of parsley

1 sprig tarragon

2 sprigs of dill

½ cup cane sugar

1 tablespoon white
    peppercorns

1 tablespoon mustard
    seeds

1–2 bay leaves

2 cloves

2 teaspoons salt

Thoroughly wash and brush the celery under cold running water. Boil the salt with the lemon juice and water, add the celery, boil again, and simmer on low heat for about 20 minutes. They should not get too soft, though. Remove the celery, let cool off, and cut julienne.

Peel the onions and cut into rings. Wash the parsley, tarragon, and dill and thoroughly dab dry. Chop finely (without the stalks) and pile into the prepared jars.

Boil the brew with the sugar, peppercorns, mustard seeds, bay leaves, and cloves and reduce for about 5 minutes. Remove the foam and fill the brew into jars. Store in a cool and dry place. Let soak for 1 month before consumption.

❯ Tip

Pickled celery is particularly delicious with the apples in lemon balm vinegar recipe on page 56.

Cocktail tomatoes

Remove the stems of the cocktail tomatoes, prick several times with a toothpick, and pack into the jars with the basil leaves. Boil the vinegar with the sugar, chili pepper, cilantro, peppercorns, allspice berries, cloves, and half the cinnamon stick. Pour the boiling-hot mixture over the tomatoes, covering by an inch. Use wooden spatula sections to hold the fruit in place and close the lid tightly. Marinate at least 4–6 weeks before serving.

3¼ cups vinegar
2 cups cocktail tomatoes
½ cup sugar
1 chili pepper
5 basil leaves
10 cilantro corns
10 black peppercorns
2 allspice berries
2 cloves
½ cinnamon stick

Cocktail tomatoes—they look as good as they taste

Mediterranean zucchini with herbs

Thinly slice the zucchini. Place on a kitchen cloth, sprinkle with salt, and let sit for 30 minutes. Pat the slices with a paper towel, turn them around, and repeat the salt process on the other side.

Heat about 3 finger-widths of oil in a large pan and deep-fry the zucchini in batches until light brown, remove with a skimmer, and drain well on paper towels. Slice the garlic thinly, add salt, and mash into a smooth paste. Chop the herbs.

Mix the wine vinegar with the salt, pepper, herbs, garlic, and olive oil. Mix the zucchini with the marinade, fill the jars, and leave in the refrigerator for 24 hours.

½ cup mild wine vinegar
1¼ cup olive oil
4 pounds zucchini
5 garlic cloves
2 teaspoons salt
5 basil leaves
1 sprig oregano
1 small bunch of parsley
salt
pepper
oil to deep-fry

❯ Tip

Use the flat side of a knife to mash the garlic into a paste.

Zucchini salad

2 cups mild vinegar
1 cup water
2 pounds zucchini
2 yellow bell peppers
3 large onions
½ cup carrots
½ cup celery
4 garlic cloves
¾ cup sugar
3 teaspoons salt
1 teaspoon mustard
   seeds
1 teaspoon allspice
   berries
1 teaspoon peppercorns
2 bay leaves
3 hyssop leaves

Finely grate the zucchini, carrots, and celery. Thinly slice the onions and bell peppers, and combine with the other vegetables. In a saucepan combine the vinegar, water, bay leaves, hyssop leaves, mustard seeds, allspice, and peppercorns. Add the vegetables and boil for 8 minutes, then fill the jars and close tightly.

Greetings from the South.

Pickled zucchini

2 cups vinegar
6 cups water
6½ pounds zucchini
3 red bell pepper
2 large onions
½ cup sugar
2–3 tablespoons salt
1 tablespoon pickling
   spices

Thinly slice the zucchini, grate the onions finely, and cut the bell peppers into rings. Combine the vegetables, add salt, mix again, and let soak for 20 minutes. Boil the vinegar, water, sugar, and pickling spices. Add the vegetables and simmer for 3 minutes. Pour the hot mixture into the jars and close tightly.

> ❯ Tip

These pickled zucchinis are a great addition to a cold snack.

Onion bell pepper pickles

Thinly slice the onions and cut the bell peppers into thin rings. Combine in a bowl and sprinkle with 4 tablespoons salt. Let sit for about 2 hours. Strain the brew, rinse the vegetables with cold water, and drain in a sieve.

Boil the vinegar, sugar, peppermint, bell pepper powder, dill seeds, and salt, and then simmer for 5 minutes. Put the vegetables into the jar and pour the boiling brew over them so they are completely covered. Close immediately and store for at least 7 days.

4¼ cups white wine
  vinegar or apple cider
  vinegar
3 pounds onions
3 red bell peppers
2 yellow bell peppers
½ cup sugar
4 tablespoons salt
2 tablespoons dried
  peppermint
2 tablespoons bell pepper
  powder
2 tablespoons dill seeds
2 teaspoons salt

Pickled zucchini (left) Onion bell pepper pickles (right)

Vinegar vegetables

2 cups white wine vinegar

1 cup water

1 small fennel bulbs

1 green bell pepper

1 red bell pepper

¾ cup cauliflower

1 cup carrots

1 garlic clove

1 tablespoon sugar

1 teaspoon black
    peppercorns

1 teaspoon mustard
    seeds

6 juniper berries

2 cloves

¼ cinnamon stick

salt as desired

saltwater

Cut the cauliflower into florets. Cut the bell pepper into rings. Cut the carrots and fennel bulb into thin slices. Fill a pot with saltwater, add the vegetables, and boil until they are firm to the bite. Remove them with a skimmer, shock under cold running water, and drain.

Fill the jars with the vegetables, either mixed or in layers. In a saucepan combine the white wine vinegar, 1 cup water, sugar, salt, peppercorns, mustard seeds, juniper berries, cinnamon stick, and cloves, and bring to a boil.

Add the finely chopped garlic and simmer until the sugar is dissolved. Taste and season. Pour into the jars and close tightly after allowing the liquid to cool. Store in a cool place for 3 weeks before serving.

❱ Tip

Vinegar vegetables are a great snack, but they can also replace a salad at lunchtime.

Ratatouille vegetables

1 tablespoon wine
    vinegar

3 tablespoons olive oil

¼ cup water (depending
    on the vegetables'
    water content)

2 yellow bell peppers

2 red bell peppers

3 medium-sized onions

4 garlic cloves

3–4 ripe tomatoes

10 fresh basil leaves

salt and pepper to taste

Cut the bell peppers, onions, and garlic into bite-size pieces. Stem and quarter the tomatoes. Wash the basil leaves under cold running water and chop finely.

In a covered pot on medium to high heat, steam the bell pepper with the tomatoes, onion, garlic, wine vinegar, olive oil, and water for about 15 minutes. Stir occasionally, and add water if necessary. Put the vegetables and basil into the jars and close tightly. Store in a cool place and serve soon.

❱ Tip

Vary the recipe according to your preferences. Try this recipe with a sprig of thyme. You can impress your guests at the cold buffet with the ratatouille vegetables. Serve them as an appetizer with thinly sliced Parma ham and finely grated parmesan. For a longer shelf life, sterilize the jars.

Piccalilli

Thinly slice the carrots and cut the cauliflower into florets. Cut the green beans into ¾-inch pieces. Peel and cut the kohlrabi into small cubes. Peel the honeydew, remove the seeds, and cut into small cubes. Wash and drain the grapes.

Put the vegetables and fruit into a large glass bowl and cover with cold water. Dissolve ⅓ cup of salt in a little hot water and add to the vegetables and fruit. Put a weight on top to keep them submerged, and let soak for 24 hours.

Strain the fruit and vegetables and rinse under cold running water, drain, and put into a large bowl. Add the coarsely ground mustard seeds.

In a saucepan, combine the spice vinegar, turmeric, and 3 tablespoons salt and boil for 10 minutes. Pour the boiling liquid over the vegetables and fruit and mix well. Put into the prepared jars and close tightly. You may consume Piccalilli right away; however, it improves with time.

4¼ cups spiced vinegar
1¾ cups carrots
½ cup green beans
1 cup cauliflower
1 cup kohlrabi
1 cup honeydew
¾ cup seedless green grapes
⅓ cup plus 3 tablespoons salt
1¾ cups yellow mustard seeds
1 tablespoon ground turmeric

❱ Tip

Taste the vegetables and fruit after soaking for 24 hours in saltwater. If they are too salty, submerge in cold water for 10 minutes. Piccalilli is an exotic side dish for cheese platters.

Vinegar vegetables (left) and Ratatouille vegetables (right)

Puszta cabbage

2 cups white wine vinegar
2 cups water
¼ cup oil
1 small cabbage head
5 green bell peppers
5 red bell peppers
2 yellow bell peppers
3 carrots
3 onions
½ cup sugar
2 tablespoons salt
1 tablespoon mustard
  seeds
1 teaspoon white pepper
1 teaspoon black
  peppercorns
3 bay leaves

Cut the bell peppers into strips and cut the onions into rings. Grind the herbs. Thinly slice the carrots. Combine all in a large bowl, add salt, and let soak overnight.

The following day, boil the white wine vinegar with the water, sugar, mustard seeds, peppercorns, and bay leaves. Press out the vegetables with your hands to soften them, add to the boiling brew and boil briefly. Remove the vegetables with a skimmer and pack tightly into the prepared jars. Boil the brew again and pour over the vegetables. Cover the surface with oil and close tightly.

❯ Tip

Vary the side dishes as you wish.

Mushrooms in vinegar

Pickled mushrooms

Clean the mushrooms and cut large ones in half or quarters. Boil in saltwater for about 4 minutes. Boil the white wine vinegar with the water, shallots, herb salt, sugar, bay leaf, tarragon, and borage for about 15 minutes. Add the mushrooms and boil for another 15 minutes. Remove with a skimmer and pile into jars. Let the brew cool down and pour over the mushrooms. Close the jars tightly and serve soon after opening.

½ cup white wine vinegar
½ cup water
2 cups small, firm
   mushrooms
2 shallots
1 sprig tarragon
1 leaf of borage
½ teaspoon herb salt
1 pinch of sugar
1 bay leaf

Pickled mushrooms—a light, wholesome appetizer or side dish

Eggs in vinegar

Quail eggs in vinegar marinade

1¾ cup white wine
  vinegar
10 quail eggs
1 onion
 2–3 pieces of pickled
   piri piri
2 sprigs tarragon
⅓-inch fresh ginger root
1 teaspoon white
  peppercorns

Hard-boil the quail eggs for about 3 minutes and put into a jar with the tarragon. Peel the onion and cut into rings. Cut the peeled ginger root into thin slices. Bring the white wine vinegar, onion rings, and ginger slices to a boil and add the peppercorns. Cool to room temperature, then pour the vinegar brew over the eggs. Keep in the refrigerator and consume within a week.

❱ Tip

Eggs in vinegar marinade are particularly decorative on cold platters, and they taste great.

Pickled quail eggs—a special delicacy

Fish in vinegar

Pickled herring in cream sauce

Cover the herring with water and let sit in a cool place for about 6 hours. Change the water once or twice during this period. Then rinse, pat dry, and put into a bowl.

Peel the onions and cut into thin rings. Peel, pare, and thinly slice the apples. Drain the gherkins and cut into thin slices. Combine the onions, apples, and gherkins with the bay leaves, peppercorns, and mustard seeds and pile over the herring.

Mix the apple cider vinegar with the sour cream and pour over herring mixture. Cover and let soak for 2–3 days in the refrigerator before serving. This delicacy is meant for eating soon.

❱ Tip

Bismarck herring in cream sauce can be seasoned with salt, pepper, or sugar before serving.

6 tablespoons apple cider vinegar
1½ cups sour cream
16 salted herring filets
4 onions
1 sour apple
2 gherkins
3 small bay leaves
1 teaspoon colored peppercorns
1 teaspoon mustard seeds

Fried herring

Descale and clean the herring, rinse, and pat dry with a paper towel. Remove the heads, fry in butter until golden-brown on both sides, and place in a bowl.

Peel the onion and cut into rings. Boil the white wine vinegar with the water, salt, sugar, peppercorns, and bay leaves. Cool the marinade completely and pour over the fish. Let soak in the fridge for a day before serving. Consume soon.

3¼ cups white wine vinegar
1 cup water
10 green herrings
1 large onion
½ cup butter
4 teaspoons salt
1 teaspoons sugar
10 peppercorns
2 bay leaves

Herring in cream sauce

Rinse the herring, pay dry, and cut into bite-sized pieces.

Cut the onion into thin rings and blanch for about 2 minutes. Place alternating layers of onion rings, allspice berries, and bay leaves into the jars, topping off with the onion rings.

Combine the cream, white wine vinegar, and sugar, and pour over the filets. Close tightly and marinate in the refrigerator for 2 days. Consume soon.

1 cup white wine vinegar
1¼ cup cream
12 cleaned herring filets
2 large onions
1 tablespoon sugar
7 allspice berries
2 bay leaves

Herring in mustard sauce

1 cup white wine vinegar

6 whole salted herrings
   or 12 prepared herring
   filets

3 onions

4 eggs

1 teaspoon colored
   peppercorns

2 tablespoons mustard
   powder

1½ tablespoons sugar

3 cloves

1 bay leaf

½ teaspoon ground
   turmeric

In a saucepan, bring the white wine, cloves, bay leaf, and peppercorns to a boil, and then simmer for a few minutes. Cool completely. Thinly slice the onions and blanch for about 2 minutes. Rinse the filets, pat dry, and cut into bite-sized pieces.

Mix together the eggs, sugar, mustard powder, and turmeric, and add to the vinegar brew. Stir this mixture over a steam bath until it thickens and coats the back of a spoon. Then pour over the onions and let cool. Mix the herring pieces with the egg-onion-mustard sauce, fill into jars, close tightly, and store in a cool place for 3 days before serving. Use soon.

Herring with carrots and leek

1 cup white wine vinegar

1 cup water

8 herring filets

2 carrots

2 onions

1 leek

¾ cup sugar

1 teaspoon colored
   peppercorns

1 teaspoon mustard
   seeds

½ teaspoon dried thyme

1 bay leaf

If you are using fresh, green herring, cut into filets and remove the bones. If you are using salted herring filets, rinse them with water and store in the refrigerator for at least 12 hours. Change the water once or twice.

Rinse the fish filets, pat dry, and cut into pieces. Place the filets and vegetables into the jars in alternating layers, and add thyme. Boil the white wine vinegar, water, sugar, peppercorns, allspice, and bay leaf for 2 minutes, then cool completely. Fill the jars with the brew and marinate—2 days for the salted herring, 3 days for the green herring. Store in the refrigerator and consume soon.

> ❭ Tip

If you use salted herring, reduce the amount of sugar as desired. We recommend 2 tablespoons of sugar.

Marinated herring

Cover the salted herring with water and store in the refrigerator for at least 12 hours, changing the water once or twice. Then rinse the filets, pat dry, and cut into ¾-inch pieces. Peel the shallots and cut into rings.

In a saucepan, combine the white wine vinegar, water, sugar, mustard seeds, peppercorns, and bay leaf. Bring to a boil for 2 minutes and let cool completely. Place the filets, alternating with the shallot rings, into jars, close tightly, and let marinate in the refrigerator for 1–2 days before serving. Consume soon.

1 cup white wine vinegar
1 cup water
8 salted herring filets
3 cups shallots
1 cup sugar
1 teaspoons mustard
   seeds
5 white peppercorns
1 bay leaf

Bell pepper herring

If you use fresh, green herring, cut them into filets and remove the bones. If you use salted herring, cover with cold water for at least 12 hours, changing the water once or twice.

Rinse the fish filets, pat dry, and cut into pieces. Peel the onion and cut into rings. Cut the bell pepper into strips and layer the onions and bell peppers with the filet pieces in jars. In a saucepan, combine the white wine vinegar, water, sugar, bay leaf, mustard seeds, and peppercorns and bring to a boil. Simmer for 2 minutes and let cool. Pour the cooled marinade over the bell pepper herring and marinate 1–2 days (salted herring) or 3 days (green herring) in the refrigerator. Serve soon.

1 cup white wine vinegar
1 cup water
8 herring filets
2 onions
2 red bell peppers
¾ cup sugar
1 teaspoon mustard
   seeds
1 teaspoon colored
   peppercorns
1 bay leaf

Spicy rollmops

1 cup white wine vinegar
10 green herrings
⅓ cup shallots
⅓ cup capers
2 gherkins
3 teaspoons salt
3 teaspoons spicy-hot
  mustard
10 black peppercorns
2 bay leaves
½ teaspoons sugar

Cover the herring with water and refrigerate for at least 12 hours, changing the water once or twice.

Drain the herring, pat dry, and cut into filets. To do this, remove the head and tail fin. Starting from the back, cut the fish along its spine and along the belly toward the head. Use a sharp knife to remove the spine. Cut the filet lengthwise at the center and make sure the skin is not damaged. Carefully remove the skin, rinse, and pat dry.

Peel and finely chop the shallots. Cut the gherkins into small cubes. Mix the shallots with the gherkins and capers and rub into the herring filets, roll them up, and fasten with a toothpick. Pile the rollmops into jars and add the bay leaves and peppercorns.

Boil the white wine vinegar with the sugar and salt, cool completely, and pour over the rollmops. Close the jars tight and refrigerate at least 1 week before serving.

Sherry herrings (left)
Spicy-hot rollmops (right)

Sherry herring

Clean the herring: Remove the bones and dark inner skins. Remove the heads, tails, and fins and let soak in cold water for at least 12 hours. Remove the herring, pat dry, and cut into pieces.

Dissolve the sugar in the red wine vinegar and sherry, add the pepper and olive oil, and mix with the herring pieces. Slice the onions into rings and chop the garlic. Drain and slice the olives. Rinse the thyme under cold water and pat dry.

Combine the onion rings, garlic, olive slices, thyme, peppers, and fish. Fill the jars and close tightly. Store in the refrigerator and consume within 1 week.

5 tablespoons red wine vinegar
1 cup dry sherry
3 tablespoons olive oil
2¼ pounds salted herring
2 small red onions
3 garlic cloves
⅓ cup olives stuffed with bell pepper
1 sprig thyme
1 tablespoon sugar
1 teaspoon coarsely ground black pepper
1 small dried pepper

Swedish herring

Cover the salted herring with water and refrigerate at least 12 hours. Change the water once or twice. Boil the white wine vinegar with the water, sugar, allspice, bay leaves, and mustard seeds, and cool.

Slice the onions into rings. Peel and slice the carrots. Peel the ginger root and radish and cut into small cubes. Drain the herring, pat dry, and cut into filets. To do this, remove the head and tail, pull the belly sections apart, and place the fish on a work surface with the skin up. Slide your thumb firmly along the spine to loosen it. Turn the fish around and pull out the bones in one piece.

Cut the herring into about ¾-inch pieces and place in a prepared jar along with the carrots, ginger, and radish. Pour in enough cold marinade to cover the fish and vegetables.

Close the jar tightly and marinate in the refrigerator for 2–3 days.

1 cup white wine vinegar
1 cup water
4 salted herrings (½ pound each)
1 cup carrots
4 red onions
1½ inches fresh radish
⅓-inch fresh ginger root
½ cup sugar
2 teaspoons mustard seeds
10 allspice berries
2 bay leaves

❱ Tip

Served with bread or fried potatoes, these Swedish herrings are a rather unusual and delicious meal.

2 cups apple cider vinegar

2 cups dry white wine

8 whole salted herrings

6 tablespoons spicy-hot mustard

4 large pickled mustard gherkins

1 large onion

2 tablespoons capers

2 teaspoons juniper berries

1 teaspoons allspice berries

2 cloves

Rollmops in white wine marinade

Cover the salted herring with water and store in the refrigerator for at least 12 hours. Change the water once or twice.

Mash the juniper berries, allspice berries, and cloves. Boil the apple cider vinegar with the white wine, juniper berries, allspice berries, and cloves for about 10 minutes. Let the marinade cool down completely. Drain the herring, pat dry, and cut into filets. Remove the head and tail, pull the belly sections apart, and place on a work surface with the skin up. Firmly run your thumb along the spine to loosen it. Turn the fish around and pull out the bones in one piece.

Place the herring skin side down onto a board and rub with mustard. Thinly slice the onions and blanch in boiling water for a few seconds. Cut the pickled gherkins into thin strips and into pieces the same width as the herring filets. Place one piece of gherkin onto the wide section of the herring filet, add a few onion rings and capers, roll up, and fasten with toothpicks.

Stack the rollmops with the remaining onions into the jars, topping off with a layer of onions. Fill the jars with marinade so that the onions are covered completely. Close tightly and store in a cool place for about 1 week.

❯ Tip

Instead of salted herring you can also use whole matie double filets. This will eliminate the work of cutting them into filets, and you only need to rinse the double filets and dab them dry before preparation.

Preparing spicy-hot rollmops

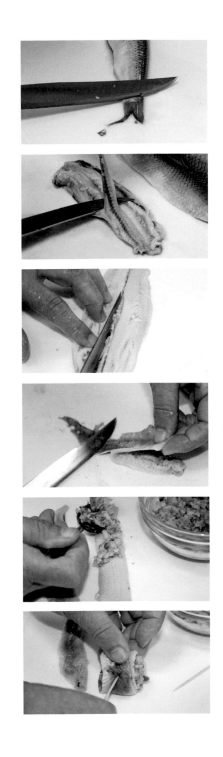

Remove the herring's head and tail. Cut the fish along the spine and the belly towards the head.

Use a sharp knife to remove the spine.

Cut the filets in half lengthwise and make sure the skin is not damaged.

Carefully remove the skin, rinse, and pat dry.

Place on a work surface and add filling to about half the filet. Roll up tightly starting from the filling end.

Fasten with a toothpick.

Marinated trout

4 small trout (cleaned)

2 tablespoons lemon juice

2 tablespoons flour

4 tablespoons canola oil

½ pound onions

1¼ cup water

1¼ cup white wine vinegar

1 tablespoon dried dill

2 bay leaves

1 tablespoon mustard seeds

2 teaspoon sugar

1 chili pod

salt

Remove the heads and fins of the trout, rinse, pat dry, add the lemon juice, and let soak for 10 minutes. Dredge in flour, fry both sides in canola oil, and place in a bowl. Thinly slice the onion and boil with the white wine vinegar, herbs, and spices. Let the brew cool and pour over the warm fish so they are covered. Marinate in the refrigerator for 1 day and enjoy.

❱ Tip

Char or whitefish may be substituted for trout.

Pickled salmon (left) and Marinated trout (right)

Pickled salmon

Thinly slice the onions. Cut the salmon filet into one-inch-wide pieces. Put half the onion slices into a pot and place the salmon on top. Add 1 teaspoon salt and the juice of half a lemon and cover with water. Slowly bring to a boil and let simmer for 1 minute. Remove the salmon from the pot and layer into a jar with the remaining raw onion slices. The last layer should consist of onions.

Strain the brew in a pot and reduce somewhat. Add the white wine vinegar, sugar, peppercorns, mustard seeds, dill seeds, cloves, and the remaining salt, and boil for 2–3 minutes. Pour the hot brew into the jar so the ingredients are completely covered. Close tightly and store in a cold place for 3 days before serving.

¼ cup white wine vinegar
1 pound salmon filet
2 small onions
½ lemon
2 tablespoons sugar
1½ teaspoon salt
1 tablespoon black peppercorns
½ teaspoon mustard seeds
½ teaspoon dill seeds
3 cloves

> **Tip**

Pike and whitefish are suitable substitutes for salmon in this recipe. There is no need to remove the bones, as they turn soft and edible during pickling.

Danish burgundy matie

Put the matie filets into cold water—the duration depends on their salt content. If it is low, 1 hour is sufficient, but several hours may be required.

Peel the onions and cut into rings. Briefly boil the red wine with the red wine vinegar, sugar, peppercorns, mustard seeds, juniper berries, cloves, bay leaves, ginger, and chili pod. Add the onion rings and simmer for another 5 minutes. Let the marinade cool.

Meanwhile, drain the filets and put into the prepared jars, either whole or cut into pieces. Pour the cold marinade over the maties so they are completely covered. Close tightly and marinate for 2 days before serving. Use within 1 week.

1 cup red wine vinegar
1 cup red burgundy
6–8 matie filets
4 small red onions
¾ cups sugar
1 teaspoon black peppercorns
½ teaspoon mustard seeds
4 juniper berries
2 cloves
2 bay leaves
⅓-inch dried ginger root
1 small dried chilli pod

> **Tip**

Serve with bread for a delicious meal.

Fish pickles

4¼ cups white wine vinegar

6 tablespoon peanut oil, divided

2¼ pounds firm, fresh fish filets (monkfish, haddock, or mackerel)

1 pound onions

¾-inch fresh ginger root

2 dried chili pods

2 tablespoons brown sugar

1 tablespoon curry powder

5 teaspoons sea salt, divided

1 teaspoons ground turmeric

2 small bay leaves

Cut the fish filets into pieces, mix with 3 teaspoons sea salt, and let soak in a cool place for 2 hours. Drain and pat dry with a paper towel. Heat 4 tablespoons of the peanut oil and fry the filets for 3 minutes on each side. They should be slightly brown and just about done. Drain on a paper towel.

Thinly slice the onions and ginger root. In a saucepan, combine the onion rings, white wine vinegar, remaining sea salt, brown sugar, curry powder, turmeric, and ginger, and bring to a boil. Steam the onions until they are somewhat soft, remove with a skimmer, and drain.

Pile the filets and the onions in the jars, alternating with the chili pods and bay leaves, and ending with the onions. Boil the vinegar brew again and pour over the filets. Cover with the remaining oil, close tightly, and marinate for 2 days before serving. Store in a cool place and consume soon.

Fish pickles—a light, delicious dinner

Steeped vinegars

Basil vinegar
Boil the coarsely chopped onion, red wine vinegar, green peppercorns, and brown sugar. Put the washed basil leaves into a bottle and fill with the strained brew. Close the bottle and let sit for 1 week before using.

3¼ cups red wine vinegar
1 red onion
1 teaspoon green
   peppercorns
1 tablespoon brown sugar
2 basil leaves

Barberry vinegar
Mix the ingredients well and pour into a bottle. Leave for a few days in a light but cool place (not in the refrigerator) to soak. Barberry juice is available at specialty food stores.

½ cup white wine vinegar
¼ cup white wine
1 cup barberry juice

Dill vinegar
Briefly boil the colored peppercorns, mustard seeds, sugar, and white wine vinegar. Put the dill umbel into a bottle and pour the strained, hot brew over it. Close tightly and store for 2 weeks. Strain the vinegar again and pour into a clean bottle.

❱ Tip

Dill vinegar is a tasty addition to cucumber salad.

2 cups white wine vinegar
2 teaspoons colored
   peppercorns
1 teaspoon mustard
   seeds
2 teaspoons sugar
1 fresh dill umbel or 3 dill
   sprigs

Aromatic vinegar
Make a spice bag from the ginger root, cilantro, allspice, cinnamon stick, mace, and aniseed. In a saucepan, bring the white wine vinegar and sea salt to a boil, add the spice bag, and simmer for 10 minutes. Let the liquid cool, then remove the spice bag and strain the vinegar. Fill the prepared bottles and close tightly.

❱ Tip

You can use the aromatic vinegar right away. However, with a little patience you will notice that the vinegar gets more aromatic with time.

4¼ cups white wine
   vinegar
2 tablespoons sliced
   ginger root
1 teaspoon whole cilantro
1 teaspoon allspice
   berries
1 cinnamon stick
½ teaspoon mace
½ teaspoon aniseed
1 teaspoon sea salt

Flower vinegar

4¼ cups white wine
    vinegar
1 handful of flowers
1 clove
½ cinnamon stick

Remove the leaves from the flower stalks and put into a jar. Add the cloves and cinnamon stick and pour the white wine vinegar over it. Close the jar and let soak for 2 weeks in a sunny place. Shake the jar occasionally. Strain the vinegar into a bottle using a cheesecloth.

❱ Tip

Depending on the season, use violets, primrose, elberberry flowers, or camomile. We recommend not mixing flower varieties. Flower vinegar goes well with dandelion salad, corn salad, and spinach salad.

Apple-herb vinegar

3¼ cups apple cider
    vinegar
2 garlic cloves
2 sprigs oregano
1 sprig basil
1 tablespoon dried apple
    peels
1 teaspoon mustard
    seeds
10 colored peppercorns

Put the garlic cloves, apple peels, oregano, basil, mustard seeds, and peppercorns into a bottle. Fill with the apple cider vinegar and let soak for at least 3 weeks.

❱ Tip

Add dried apple rings to the vinegar; they enhance the fruity taste.

Flower vinegar (left)
Apple-herb vinegar (right)

Strawberry vinegar

Wash the strawberries, pat dry, mash with a fork, and put into a twist-top jar. Boil the apple cider vinegar vigorously for 1–2 minutes, cool to about 100° F, and pour over the strawberries.

　　Close the jar and leave in a warm place for about 2 weeks, stirring occasionally. Strain the vinegar and pour into a bottle. For a more intense taste, add a few strawberries and/or basil leaves on a wooden skewer. The vinegar can be used right away.

2 cups apple cider vinegar
½ pound ripe strawberries
a few small, firm strawberries and/or basil leaves for decoration

❱ Tip

Instead of strawberries, substitute the same amount of blackberries or currants.

Tarragon vinegar with raspberries

Put the washed and stemmed raspberries, raspberry leaves, and sprig of tarragon into bottles. Briefly boil the red wine vinegar, sugar, and peppercorns. Fill the bottles with the hot vinegar brew and close tightly. Let soak for 2 weeks before consumption.

3¼ cups red wine vinegar
15 raspberries
5 raspberry leaves
1 tablespoon sugar
1 teaspoon black peppercorns
1 sprig tarragon

Horseradish vinegar

Peel and slice the horseradish. Make a spice bag with the peppercorns, mustard seeds, allspice, and cinnamon stick. Combine the white wine vinegar and salt in a saucepan, bring to a boil, and simmer for 10 minutes. When cool, remove the spice bag, strain the vinegar, pour into a bottle, and close tightly. The vinegar can be used right away.

2 cups mild white wine vinegar
1 radish
5 white peppercorns
½ teaspoon mustard seeds
3 allspice berries
1 small piece of cinnamon stick
1½ teaspoons sea salt

❱ Tip

Red beet salad with horseradish vinegar is a tasty specialty.

Lime vinegar

Thoroughly brush the lime and orange under running water, and dry. Slice and seed the lime. Peel the orange thinly without removing the white skin. Put the lime slices and orange peel into a bottle and pour the apple vinegar over it. Shake well and leave in a sunny place for about 2 weeks. Strain the vinegar, pour into a clean bottle, and store in a cool place.

3¼ cups apple cider vinegar
1 lime
1 orange

Bay leaf vinegar

4¼ cups white wine
vinegar
3 garlic cloves
6 bay leaves
3 teaspoons cilantro
corns
2 dried chili pods

Peel the garlic cloves and cut in half. Mix all the ingredients and pour into the bottles. Let soak for 2 weeks, closed tightly. Strain the vinegar and pour into clean bottles.

Marjoram vinegar

1½ cup white wine
vinegar
1 shallot
1 garlic clove
8 peppercorns
2 sprigs of marjoram

Peel and cube the shallot, and boil for a few mintues with the peppercorns, coarsely chopped garlic, and white wine vinegar, then strain. Wash the marjoram and pat dry, put into a bottle, and pour the hot vinegar mix over it. Close the bottle and let soak for a few days before using.

Orange vinegar with lemon balm

1½ cup red wine vinegar
2 oranges
2 tablespoons honey
1 sprig lemon balm

Thoroughly wash one of the oranges under hot running water. Grate the peel. Press out the juice of both oranges. Boil the red wine vinegar, orange juice, and honey, stirring. Add the grated orange peel. Put the lemon balm into a bottle and pour the hot vinegar mix over it. Let soak for 10 days before consuming.

Lemon vinegar with tarragon

3¼ cups white wine
vinegar
½ cup sherry
1 lemon
1 sprig tarragon

Press out the lemon. Mix the white wine vinegar, sherry, and lemon juice. Wash the tarragon sprig, pat dry, and put into the bottle. Fill with the vinegar mix, close, and let soak for 14 days before using.

Raspberry vinegar

1 cup white wine vinegar
1 cup white wine
½ pound wild raspberries

Carefully select the wild raspberries, but do not wash. Put the fruit into a jar and pour the white wine and white wine vinegar over them. Strain the raspberries after 1 week and gently boil the raspberry vinegar for 10 minutes. Put into a bottle and close tightly.

❱ Tip

Raspberry vinegar is great on salad greens.

Rose flower vinegar

Put the unwashed rose petals into a bottle and pour the white wine vinegar over them. Shake well, close tightly and leave in a sunny place for 2 weeks. Shake the bottle now and then. Strain the vinegar with a fine cloth and pour into a clean bottle.

2 cups white wine vinegar
4 unsprayed, fully
    blooming rose petals

Raspberry vinegar (left)
Rose flower vinegar
(right)

Vinegar, Oil, and Alcohol

PICKLED

Delicacies

Pickling in Oil

Vegetables in oil

Artichokes in oil

2 cups roasted
   sesame oil
3 pounds baby artichokes
1 large lemon
1 untreated large lemon
1 tablespoon salt
1 tablespoon finely
   chopped thyme

Grate the peel of the untreated lemon, and press out both lemons. Put the pressed-out halves aside. Mix the salt, lemon juice, and lemon peel in a large bowl and stir to dissolve the salt. Cut off the artichoke stems and remove the leaves. Cut in a way that the heart is exposed. Immediately rub the heart with the lemon juice to avoid discoloration. Use a sharp spoon to remove the prickly hairs. Put the artichokes into a bowl with the lemon juice mix and marinade for 30 minutes. Pile them into the jar. Mix the oil with the lemon marinade and pour it into the jar. Close tightly and let sit for 6–8 weeks, shaking occasionally.

Artichokes in oil—only the artichoke flesh at the bottom is used.

Preparing the artichokes

Use a sharp knife to cut off the stem (as close to the bottom as possible).

Pluck the leaves.

Strip off the leaves until the inner core is laid bare. Rub with lemon juice so it will not turn brown. Cut the bottom of the artichoke heart so that it is flat and remove the hard sections. Rub the cut surfaces with lemon.

Scrape out the prickly bits with a small spoon from the center of the heart.

Eggplant in oil

2 cups olive oil
2¼ pounds baby eggplant
¾ cup pecans
2 untreated lemons
10 small garlic cloves
1 teaspoon salt

Remove the stem from the eggplant and steam for 5–7 minutes until they are somewhat soft. Let cool. Halve the pecans. Cut the lemons in half lengthwise and into thin slices. Cut the garlic cloves into thin slices.

Cut into each eggplant deeply, lengthwise, and pull apart, sprinkle the inside with salt, and fill with half a nut, a lemon slice, and a few garlic slices. Close with toothpicks. Place the eggplants in the jars and put the remaining lemon slices and garlic slices between them. Heat the olive oil to 175° F and carefully pour into the jar until the eggplants are covered. Close the jar and let soak for 3–4 weeks before serving.

Mushrooms in spicy marinade

7 tablespoons
   sunflower oil
2 cups very small
   mushrooms
2 garlic cloves
peel of 1 untreated lemon
2 tablespoons lemon
   juice
½ teaspoon sugar
½ teaspoon salt
1 bay leaf
6 peppercorns
2 tablespoons chopped
   parsley

Clean the mushrooms. Peel and slice the garlic cloves. Heat the sunflower oil with the lemon juice, lemon peel, sugar, salt, bay leaf, peppercorns, garlic cloves, and parsley, while stirring. Add the mushrooms and steam in the closed pot for about 5 minutes. Stir so that the marinade and mushrooms mix well. Cool, pour into a jar, and close tightly. This mixture will last up to a week in the refrigerator.

❯ Tip

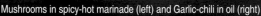

Mushrooms in spicy marinade are a wonderful side dish for cold platters and grilled meats.

Mushrooms in spicy-hot marinade (left) and Garlic-chili in oil (right)

Garlic-chili in oil

Boil the peeled garlic cloves and chili pods with the water, white wine vinegar, salt, sugar and bay leaf for 4 minutes and strain. Put the garlic cloves, chili pods, rosemary sprig, and bay leaf into a jar. Add the olive oil and tap the jar on the counter so the air bubbles can escape. Close tightly and store in a cool place.

> ❭ Tip
> _____
> Don't worry—heating and pickling the garlic and chili in oil removes much of their spicyness.

1 cup olive oil
2 cups water
½ cup white wine vinegar
4 fresh chili pods
1¼ cups garlic cloves
1 bay leaf
1 sprig rosemary
2 tablespoons salt
1 teaspoon sugar

Garlic in olive oil

Blanch the peeled garlic cloves in water, salt, and vinegar for 5 minutes. Strain the garlic cloves, let dry on a cloth, and place in a jar with the thyme, oregano, and cumin. Add the olive oil, then tap the jar on the counter so the air bubbles can escape. Close tightly and store in a cool place.

1 cup olive oil
2 cups garlic cloves
1 teaspoon thyme
1 teaspoon oregano
1 teaspoon cumin
4¼ cups water
1 tablespoon vinegar
1 tablespoon salt

Oven-dried tomatoes

Halve the tomatoes. Place with the cut side up on a baking sheet covered with aluminum foil and sprinkle with salt, sugar, and basil. Pour 4 tablespoons of olive oil over them. Preheat the oven to 175° F and roast the tomatoes for 8–12 hours, leaving the oven door slightly ajar. The tomatoes should be dry but still pliable.

Peel and thinly slice the garlic. Put the dried tomatoes, rosemary, and garlic slices into a jar and add olive oil. Close the jar and let the tomatoes soak for at least 2 days before using.

olive oil to fill the jars
4 tablespoons olive oil
2¼ pounds tomatoes
2 tablespoons salt
1 tablespoons sugar
1 tablespoons dried basil
1 sprig rosemary
2 garlic cloves

Tomatoes with cream cheese filling

2 cups cocktail tomatoes

7 ounces herbed cream cheese

1 garlic clove

6 basil leaves

salt

pepper

¾ cup olive oil

Wash the tomatoes and cut off the top. Remove the pulp with a teaspoon and season the tomatoes' inner sides with salt and pepper. Fill the tomatoes with cream cheese. Thinly slice the garlic. Put the filled tomatoes into a jar. Add the garlic and basil leaves and pour the olive oil over it so the tomatoes are covered. Close the jar and leave to soak in the refrigerator for about 2 days. It can be stored for about 1 week.

❯ Tip

The herb cream cheese can be replaced with curd or sheep or goat cream cheese.

Wild garlic pesto

1 large bunch wild garlic

½ cup almonds

4 garlic cloves

1¼ teaspoons salt

¼ cup canola oil

Blanch the almonds, peel, and grate finely. Wash the wild garlic leaves and chop finely. Peel and mince the garlic and blend with the remaining ingredients. Spoon the paste into small jars and close.

Tomatoes with cream cheese filling (left)
Wild garlic pesto (right)

Pickled peppers

In a saucepan combine the olive oil, white wine vinegar, salt, peppercorns, and peeled garlic cloves. Bring to a boil and add the peppers, boiling vigorously until the peppers are tender, then let cool completely. Remove the peppers with a skimmer and spoon into a jar. Boil the vinegar-oil mix again and let cool. Fill the jar and close tightly. Store the peppers in a dark place for a few weeks before serving.

1 cup olive oil
1 cup white wine vinegar
10 chili peppers
2 garlic cloves
1 teaspoon salt
5 black peppercorns

Pickled bell pepper with feta cheese

Preheat the oven to 400° F.

Wash the bell peppers, place on a baking pan with oil, and roast for about 20 minutes, turning often. When the skin is blistered and charred, remove them from the oven and place them in a brown paper bag to cool. Cut the bell peppers in half, and remove the seeds and stem. Use a small knife to carefully remove the skin. Cut the feta cheese into small cubes.

Peel the onions and garlic cloves and chop coarsely. Wash the chili peppers and dab dry. Press out the lemons. Pile the bell pepper, feta cheese, onions, garlic, and chili pods into jars and season with the lemon juice. Add the olive oil, close tightly and store in the refrigerator.

olive oil to fill the jars
3 red bell peppers
3 green bell peppers
2 cups feta cheese
½ pound onions
2 red chili pods
4 garlic cloves
2 lemons

❯ Tip

Leave the skin on if it is difficult to remove. However, do not skip the roasting, as it intensifies the flavor.

Pickled peppers (left)
Pickled bell pepper with feta cheese (right)

Preparing the bell pepper

Wash the bell peppers, place on a baking pan with oil and fry at about 400° F in a pre-heated oven for 20 minutes, turning often.

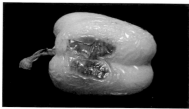

The peppers are done when the skin blisters and turns dark.

Place the hot peppers in a freezer bag or brown paper bag and let cool.

Cut the pepper in half and remove the seeds and stem.

Use a small knife to carefully remove the skin.

Halve the peppers again.

Pickled mushrooms

In a saucepan, combine the white wine vinegar, water, peeled garlic clove, salt, peppercorns, and 1 sprig of thyme. Bring to a boil and the simmer for 30 minutes. Add the mushrooms and cook for 10 minutes. Remove the mushrooms with a skimmer and drain. Spoon into a jar with the lemon peel, bay leaf, and the remaining thyme sprig.

Heat the olive oil to 170° F and pour it over the mushrooms. Close tightly and let sit for 2 weeks before serving.

1 cup olive oil
½ cup white wine vinegar
¼ cup water
2 cups mixed mushrooms
1 garlic clove
½ teaspon salt
3 black peppercorns
2 sprigs thyme, divided
1 piece of untreated
    lemon peel
1 bay leaf

Pure mushroom
deliciousness

Cheese in oil

Mozzarella in soy oil

1¾ cup soybean oil
1 pound fresh mozzarella
3 chili peppers
3 garlic cloves
1 tablespoon black
   peppercorns
1 tablespoon mustard
   seeds
2 sprigs lemon thyme
2 sprigs rosemary
peel of ½ an orange

Drain the mozzarella and cut into nut-sized pieces. Seed the peppers and cut into rings. Slice the garlic. Carefully mix the washed and dried herbs with the mozzarella, pepper rings, garlic slices, lemon peel, peppercorns, and mustard seeds, and place in a wide-mouth jar. Fill with the soy oil so the ingredients are covered. Close the jar and store in a cool, dark place. Use within 1 week.

> ❭ Tip

This recipe is great using mini-mozzarella balls or goat cheese. If you like, put some balsamic vinegar on the cheese before serving.

Goat cheese provençal

2 cups olive oil
2 cups small goat cheese
   balls or cubes
3 small onions
2 garlic cloves
1 chili pod
1 tablespoon dried
   provençal herbs
1 teaspoon juniper
   berries
1 teaspoon black
   peppercorns

Peel the garlic cloves and onions and cut into quarters. Wash the chili pod and cut into pieces. Place the goat cheese, garlic cloves, onion quarters, chili pieces, and spices in alternating layers in a large jar. Cover with the olive oil. Close the jar and store in the refrigerator for 2 days before serving. Use within 2 weeks.

> ❭ Tip

Try this recipe with feta cheese.

Pickled feta cheese

2 cups olive oil
1¾ feta cheese
½ red bell pepper
½ yellow bell pepper
3 sprigs tarragon
1 teaspoon caraway
1 teaspoon black
   peppercorns

Wash and seed the bell pepper and cut into slices. Grind half of the peppercorns. Mix the olive oil, bell pepper strips, caraway, and the whole and ground peppercorns. Cut the feta cheese into pieces, pile with the tarragon into a jar, and fill with the olive oil mix so the ingredients are covered. Close tightly and let soak in the refrigerator for at least 1 week before consumption.

Schlierbacher in a jar

Peel the onions and the garlic, cut the onions into rings and cut the garlic into pieces. Place the whole piece of cheese into the jar and add mustard seeds.

Mix together the onion rings, garlic pieces, peppercorns, dill, and tarragon. Add the mixture to the jar and cover with soy oil. Close the jar and store in a cool place for about 1 week before serving.

soy oil (to fill)

3 pieces of Schlierbacher cheese or 1 pound of other mild semi-soft cheese

2 red onions

3 garlic cloves

1 teaspoon mustard seeds

1 teaspoon white peppercorns

½ teaspoon dried dill

½ teaspoon dried tarragon

Beer cheese in canola oil

Cut the beer cheese into large pieces and put into a wide-mounth jar. Add the drained peppers, peppercorns, oregano, bay leaf, and mashed juniper berries. Cover with the canola oil. Tap the jar on the counter so the air bubbles can escape. Close tightly and store in a cool place.

canola oil to fill the jars

1¾ pound beer cheese

4 pickled red peppers

1 teaspoon green peppercorns

1 teaspoon black peppercorns

1 teaspoon ground oregano

4 juniper berries

2 bay leaves

Schlierbacher in a jar (left)
Beer cheese in canola oil (right)

Marinated feta cheese with prosciutto

9 ounces firm feta cheese
prosciutto
2 green peppers
3 garlic cloves
1 sprig peppermint
1 sprig rosemary
3 white peppercorns
1¼ cups olive oil

Cut the feta cheese into 1-inch cubes and wrap with bacon strips. Wash the peppers, remove the seeds, and cut into rings. Peel the garlic and cut into thin slices. Place the prosciutto-wrapped cheese cubes, peppers, garlic, herbs, and peppercorns into a jar. Fill with olive oil and close. Consume soon.

Camembert in a jar

sunflower oil to fill the jars
5 ounces Camembert
1 red onion
1 fresh red pepper
1 teaspoon colored
    peppercorns
1 teaspoon mustard
    seeds

Divide the Camembert and put into a jar. Peel the onion and cut into rings. Place the onion rings, peppers, peppercorns, and mustard seeds into the jar. Fill with the sunflower oil, close tightly and store in the refrigerator.

Camembert in a jar (left) and Marinated feta cheese with prosciutto (right)

Fish in oil

Seafood in oil

Wash the lemon, cut into thin slices, mix with 1 tablespoon salt, and let soak for 1 hour. Wash the fennel bulb, remove any brown sections, and thinly slice. Make a spice bag from the lemon or orange peel, bay leaf, peppercorns, and fennel seeds. Boil the white wine with the water, white wine vinegar, fennel slices, 2 teaspoons salt, and the spice bag, and simmmer at low heat for 20 minutes.

Add the squid and boil until soft, about 20 minutes. Add the scallops and boil for another 5 minutes. Remove the seafood and fennel slices with a skimmer and drain in a sieve.

Combine the warm seafood and fennel with the lemon slices, chili pods, rosemary, and remaining bay leaf and place in a jar. Heat the olive oil to 140° F and pour it over the seafood mixture to cover. Close the jar and refrigerate.

> ❱ Tip

This dish can be consumed right away.

2 cups olive oil
1 cup dry white wine
1 cup white wine vinegar
1 cup water
2 teaspoons salt
5 ounces squid
3–4 ounces scallops
1 small fennel bulb
1 lemon
2–3 pieces of lemon or orange peel
1 tablespoon salt
1 teaspoon black peppercorns
1 teaspoon fennel seeds
2 dried red chili pods
2 sprigs of rosemary
2 bay leaves

Seafood in oil
—a delicacy.

Steeped oils

Chili oil

2 cups sunflower or
   soy oil
6 dried red chili pods
1 teaspoon fennel seeds

Wash the chili pods, pat dry, and place in a bottle with the fennel seeds. Fill with the sunflower or soy oil, close tightly, and store in a cool, dark place. Marinate for 2–3 weeks, then strain and pour into a clean bottle.

Dill-juniper oil

3¼ cups sunflower oil
1 tablespoon juniper
   berries
1 tablespoon dried dill

Put the dill and juniper berries into a bottle and fill with the sunflower oil. Close tightly and store in a cool place.

Grill oil

3¼ cups canola oil
2 tablespoons sweet
   paprika
2 teaspoons white pepper
1 teaspoon curry powder
1 pinch of cayenne
   pepper

Mix the paprika, pepper, curry powder, and cayenne pepper with 6 tablespoons of the canola oil and pour into a bottle. Gradually add the remaining canola oil and shake occasionally. Close tightly and let sit for at least 2 weeks before using.

❱ Tip

This oil will get everybody's attention during the grilling season. It is excellent for marinating grilled meats and can be used throughout the year to season pork.

Spicy-hot chili pods add pizzazz to many pickled delicacies.

Lavender oil

Dry the lavender and sage leaf for 2–3 days in a well-ventilated area. Put into a bottle and pour the canola oil over it. Close tightly and store in a cool place.

1½ cups canola oil
1 dried sage leaf
1 sprig dried lavender

Lavender lemon balm oil

Put the dried lavender and the lemon balm leaves into a bottle and fill with the corn oil. Close tightly and store in a dark, cool place. Let sit for 2 weeks, then strain and pour into a clean bottle.

1½ cup corn oil
2 large sprigs of dried lavender
15 dried leaves of lemon balm

Lavender oil

Bay leaf oil

3¼ cups olive oil
5 black peppercorns
5 bay leaves

Put the dried bay leaves and peppercorns into bottles and fill with the olive oil. Close tightly and store in a cool place.

> **》 Tip**

Use this oil for potato or lentil salad.

Lime oil

2 cups sunflower oil or
light olive oil
2 limes or lemons

Wash the limes with hot water, dry well, and cut in a spiral as thinly as possible (without nicking the white inner skin). Close the jar and store in a cool place.

Lime oil (left)
Porcini mushroom oil (right)

Herb oil provençal

Peel the garlic cloves, mash, and put into a bottle with the provençal herbs. Fill with the olive oil, close, and let soak for at least 1 week. Strain the oil and pour into a clean bottle. Close tightly and store in a cool place.

2 cups cold-pressed
  olive oil
2 garlic cloves
2 tablespoons dried
  provençal herbs

Rosemary oil

Put the dried rosemary sprigs and chili pod into a bottle and fill with the olive oil. Close tightly and store in a cool place for 2–3 weeks. Strain the oil, pour into clean bottles, and store in a cool place.

3¼ cups light olive oil
1 red chili pod
2 dried rosemary sprigs

Sage oil

Put the sage leaves, chili pod, and bay leaf into a bottle and fill with the corn oil. Shake well and store in a cool place. Let soak for 2 weeks, then strain and pour into a clean bottle.

3¼ cups corn germ oil
1 bay leaf
1 chili pod
10 dried sage leaves

❱ Tip

If you want to use the sage oil for frying meats, replace the corn oil with canola oil.

Porcini mushroom oil

Briefly rinse the dried porcini mushrooms with hot water and dry thoroughly. Put the mushrooms and thyme or chervil sprig into a bottle with a wide opening. Fill with the canola oil and close tightly. Store in a cool, dark place for 2–3 weeks before using.

2 cups canola oil
0.7 ounces dried porcini
  mushrooms
1 small sprig dried thyme
  or chervil

❱ Tip

Use the mushroom oil to marinate leaf and potato salads or to marinate and fry tender meats.

Wok oil

Peel the garlic cloves and ginger and cut into thin slices. Put the garlic, ginger, and coriander seeds into a bottle and fill with the oils. Let soak for 3 weeks and strain.

1¾ cup canola oil
¼ cup sesame oil
3 garlic cloves
¾-inch fresh ginger
1 teaspoon coriander
  seeds

Spicy bell pepper oil

2 cups sunflower oil
½ cup red wine vinegar
1 red bell pepper
3 garlic cloves
1 teaspoon green
    peppercorns
1 dried rosemary sprig

Wash and halve the red bell pepper, remove seeds, and cut into 1-inch pieces. Peel and halve the garlic cloves. Loosely spear the bell pepper and garlic pieces, alternating, on a wooden skewer.

Heat the red wine vinegar, add the rosemary and peppercorn, and soak for 5 minutes. Remove the spices and drain well. Place the bell pepper-garlic skewer, rosemary, and peppercorns into a tall jar or bottle with a wide opening. Fill with the sunflower oil, close tightly, and let sit for 1 week before using.

> ❯ Tip

Use olive oil and red peppercorns if you wish. This recipe is ideal for marinating meats.

Cinnamon oil

2 cups peanut oil
1 lemon
2 cinnamon sticks

Wash and dry the lemon and peel thinly. Put the cinnamon sticks and lemon peel into a bottle and fill with peanut oil. Close the jar and store in a cool place.

Spice oil

3¼ cups olive oil
1 teaspoon white
    peppercorns
5 allspice berries
2 cloves
1 bay leaf
1 dried rosemary sprig
2 dried thyme sprigs

Put the dried herbs, peppercorns, allspice berries, bay leaf, and cloves into a bottle and fill with olive oil. Close tightly and store in a cool place.

Pickling in Sugar

Vegetables in sugar

Shallots in syrup

4¼ cups preserving sugar
6⅓ cups white wine
   vinegar
3 pounds shallots
½ cup salt
3 strips of lemon peel
1 tablespoon caraway
1 tablespoon cloves
½ dried chili pod
2 cinnamon sticks
4 cardamom pods

Peel the shallots and blanch in boiling water for a few minutes. To keep them from falling apart, don't cut the root end. Dissolve the salt in a bowl of cold water and add the shallots. Put a weight on them and let soak for 24 hours.

Prepare a spice sack with the lemon peel, caraway, cloves, cinnamon sticks, cardamom pods, and chili pods. Boil the white wine vinegar with the preserving sugar and the spice bag for 10 minutes, stirring. Remove the spice bag.

Strain the shallots and rinse under cold running water, and drain. Carefully place into the boiling syrup, briefly boil, and simmer at low heat for 15 minutes. Remove from the stove and let soak overnight.

Boil again the following day and simmer for 2 hours, until the shallots are glassy brown. Carefully remove the shallots and put them in the prepared jars. Boil the syrup vigorously for 5 minutes and pour into the jars. Close tightly. You can enjoy the shallots in syrup right away, and they get better with time.

❯ Tip

This recipe is not a quick one, but your efforts will be worthwhile. It makes an unusual, delicious side dish for venison and lamb.

Eggplant in syrup

Peel and slice the lemon. Clean the ginger root and grate finely. Remove the green leaf at the base of the eggplant, but don't cut off the stem. Perforate each eggplant several times, put into a large bowl, sprinkle with salt, and let soak for a few hours while covered. Thoroughly rinse under cold running water.

Boil water in a pot, add the eggplant, bring to a boil again and simmer for 5 minutes. Remove the vegetables and drain. Boil the preserving sugar with the lemon juice, stirring to dissolve the sugar. Add the lemon peel, ginger, cloves, and cinnamon stick and boil for 5 minutes. Add the eggplant to the boiling syrup and reduce by half, stirring occasionally. The eggplants will look glassy.

Carefully remove the eggplant from the syrup and put in the prepared jars. Boil the syrup once more and pour into the jars. Close tightly. You can enjoy this dish right away; however, it becomes even more delicious with time.

4¼ cups preserving sugar
2 1/4 pounds baby eggplants
juice of 3 large lemons
peel of 1 lemon
⅓ cup ginger root
4 tablespoons salt
6 cloves
2 cinnamon sticks

❱ Tip

You may think that this combination of ingredients is rather strange. But don't hesitate to try it. This Moroccan treat is eaten with a spoon, served with tea or coffee.

Fruit in sugar

Pepper apples with strawberries

3¼ cups preserving sugar
4¼ cups water
4 pounds apples (not too
    sour)
2 pounds strawberries
juice and peel of 1 orange
juice of 1 lemon
some cold water
1 piece candied ginger
2 tablespoons green
    peppercorns

Halve the apples, remove the core, and cut into ½-inch slices. Make lemon water with cold water and lemon juice and pour it over the apple slices—they should be completely covered to keep them from turning brown.

Boil the preserving sugar with 4¼ cups of water, add the pieces of orange peel, and boil until the sugar has dissolved. Add the orange juice, peppercorns, and candied ginger.

Remove the apple slices from the lemon water and put into the brew. They should be steamed only briefly and remain firm. Remove the fruit from the liquid and drain. Wash and stem the strawberries and layer them into the jars with the apples.

Remove the ginger and orange from the brew and let it cool, then pour it into the jars. Close tightly and store in a cool place.

> ❱ Tip

Pepper apples with strawberries should be consumed soon.

Pepper apples with
strawberries —sweet
and delicious

Recipe Index